D0463948

THE LAW OF NO-FAULT INSURANCE

Second Edition

by
Margaret C. Jasper

Oceana's Legal Almanac Series:
Law for the Layperson

2002
Oceana Publications, Inc.
Dobbs Ferry, New York

Hartness Library
Vermont Technical College
One Main St.
Randolph Center, VT 05061

Information contained in this work has been obtained by Oceana Publications from sources believed to be reliable. However, neither the Publisher nor its authors guarantee the accuracy or completeness of any information published herein, and neither Oceana nor its authors shall be responsible for any errors, omissions or damages arising from the use of this information. This work is published with the understanding that Oceana and its authors are supplying information, but are not attempting to render legal or other professional services. If such services are required, the assistance of an appropriate professional should be sought.

Library of Congress Control Number: 2002101868

ISBN 0-379-11367-8

Oceana's Legal Almanac Series: Law for the Layperson
ISSN 1075-7376

©2002 by Oceana Publications, Inc.

All rights reserved. No part of this publication may be reproduced or transmitted in any form or by any means, electronic or mechanical, including photocopy, recording, xerography, or any information storage and retrieval system, without permission in writing from the publisher.

Manufactured in the United States of America on acid-free paper.

To My Husband Chris

Your love and support
are my motivation and inspiration

-and-

In memory of my son, Jimmy

Table of Contents

ABOUT THE AUTHOR iii

INTRODUCTION v

CHAPTER 1:
OVERVIEW OF AUTOMOBILE INSURANCE

The Nature of Insurance 1
The Role of the Federal Government in Insurance Legislation 1
Mandatory Automobile Insurance 2
The Automobile Insurance Policy. 2
Liability Coverage *3*
Medical Coverage. *3*
Collision Coverage *4*
Comprehensive Coverage. *4*
Uninsured Motorists Coverage *4*
Underinsured Motorists Coverage. *4*
Supplemental Coverage *4*
Exclusions and Limitations. *5*
The Cost of Automobile Insurance 5
Available Discounts. *6*
Shared Market Insurance Programs 6
Reporting the Automobile Accident 7

CHAPTER 2:
THE HISTORY AND DEVELOPMENT OF NO-FAULT AUTOMOBILE INSURANCE LAW

Traditional Tort-Based Liability System 9
Introduction of No-Fault Concept 9
Drawbacks of No-Fault System 11

CHAPTER 3:
NO-FAULT AUTOMOBILE INSURANCE SCHEMES

No-Fault Jurisdictions 13
A Pure No-Fault System. 13
Freedom of Choice 14
The Pennsylvania Statute - An Example of the Choice System . . . 14

CHAPTER 4:
COMPONENTS OF THE NO-FAULT INSURANCE SYSTEM

In General 17
Basic Economic Loss 17
Limitations on Tort Claims 18
The No Fault/Tort Liability System 19
Add-On Legislation 20

CHAPTER 5:
NO-FAULT COVERAGE ISSUES

In General 21
Covered Vehicles. 21
Covered Uses. 21
Covered Persons 22
Litigation Under the No-Fault System 22
  First Party Claim 23
  Third Party Claim 23

CHAPTER 6:
FILING THE NO-FAULT APPLICATION

In General 25
Medical Benefits 25
Lost Earnings. 26
Survivor Benefits. 27

CHAPTER 7:
TORT ACTION THRESHOLDS

In General 29
The Monetary Threshold. 29
The Verbal Threshold 29
  Out-Of-Balance No-Fault Laws 30

CHAPTER 8:
CHOICE OF LAW ISSUES

In General 33
The Most Significant Relationship Test 33
Lex Loci Contractus. 34
Lex Loci Delecti. 34

CHAPTER 9:
NO-FAULT AUTOMOBILE INSURANCE FRAUD

In General 35
The Nature of No-Fault Insurance Fraud 35
Types of Fraudulent Practices. 36
    Fraudulent Billing Practices. 36
    False Claims of Household Help 37
    False Lost Wages Claims 37
    Multiple Claims - Identity Fraud 37
Reform Measures. 37
No-Fault Insurance Fraud in New York 37

CHAPTER 10:
AUTO CHOICE REFORM ACT OF 2001

Overview 41
Reduction in Insurance Premiums. 42
Reduction in Fraudulent Claims. 42
The Tort Maintenance System 42
The Personal Injury Protection System 43
Consumer Notification Program. 43
State Regulation 43

APPENDICES

APPENDIX 1: DIRECTORY OF STATE INSURANCE DEPARTMENTS 45

APPENDIX 2: SCOPE OF AUTOMOBILE INSURANCE COVERAGE REQUIRED
BY EACH STATE 51

APPENDIX 3: STATE AUTOMOBILE INSURANCE MINIMUM
MONETARY LIABILITY CHART 55

APPENDIX 4: DIRECTORY OF STATE MOTOR VEHICLE DEPARTMENTS 59

APPENDIX 5: AVERAGE AUTOMOBILE INSURANCE PREMIUMS—
BY STATE 65

APPENDIX 6: STATES WITH HIGHEST AVERAGE AUTO LIABILITY PREMIUMS. 69

APPENDIX 7: DIRECTORY OF MAJOR CASUALTY AND PROPERTY INSURANCE COMPANIES 71

APPENDIX 8: STATES WITH HIGHEST GROWTH IN AVERAGE AUTO LIABILITY PREMIUMS (1989-1995) 77

APPENDIX 9: NUMBER OF NO-FAULT STATES AMONG TOP 10 STATES WITH MOST EXPENSIVE AUTOMOBILE INSURANCE RATES (1987-1995). 79

APPENDIX 10: NEW YORK STATE VERBAL THRESHOLD FOR RECOVERY OF NON-ECONOMIC DAMAGES 81

APPENDIX 11: NO-FAULT RESTRICTIONS ON PAIN AND SUFFERING LAWSUITS 83

APPENDIX 12: SUBROGATION AGREEMENT IN CONNECTION WITH A CLAIM UNDER MOTOR VEHICLE NO-FAULT INSURANCE LAW 85

APPENDIX 13: EXCERPTS FROM THE MICHIGAN NO-FAULT INSURANCE STATUTES 87

APPENDIX 14: NEW YORK MOTOR VEHICLE NO-FAULT INSURANCE LAW ARBITRATION REQUEST FORM 103

APPENDIX 15: SAMPLE COMPLAINT TO RECOVER NO-FAULT INSURANCE BENEFITS UNDER NEW YORK STATE LAW 105

APPENDIX 16: SAMPLE COMPLAINT FOR PERSONAL INJURY IN AN AUTOMOBILE ACCIDENT UNDER NEW YORK STATE LAW. 107

APPENDIX 17: SAMPLE APPLICATION FOR NO-FAULT BENEFITS 111

APPENDIX 18: AUTHORIZATION FOR RELEASE OF MEDICAL RECORDS IN CONNECTION WITH A CLAIM UNDER MOTOR VEHICLE NO-FAULT INSURANCE LAW 113

APPENDIX 19: VERIFICATION OF MEDICAL TREATMENT BY ATTENDING PHYSICIAN OR OTHER HEALTH CARE PROVIDER IN CONNECTION WITH A CLAIM UNDER MOTOR VEHICLE NO-FAULT INSURANCE LAW 115

APPENDIX 20: VERIFICATION OF HOSPITAL TREATMENT IN CONNECTION WITH A CLAIM UNDER MOTOR VEHICLE NO-FAULT INSURANCE LAW. 117

APPENDIX 21: AUTHORIZATION FOR RELEASE OF EMPLOYMENT INFORMATION IN CONNECTION WITH A CLAIM UNDER MOTOR VEHICLE NO-FAULT INSURANCE LAW 119

APPENDIX 22: EMPLOYER WAGE VERIFICATION REPORT IN CONNECTION
WITH A CLAIM UNDER MOTOR VEHICLE NO-FAULT INSURANCE LAW 121

APPENDIX 23: VERIFICATION OF SELF-EMPLOYMENT INCOME IN
CONNECTION WITH A CLAIM UNDER MOTOR VEHICLE NO-FAULT
INSURANCE LAW 123

APPENDIX 24: AGREEMENT TO PURSUE SOCIAL SECURITY DISABILITY
BENEFITS IN CONNECTION WITH A CLAIM UNDER MOTOR VEHICLE
NO-FAULT INSURANCE LAW 125

APPENDIX 25: AUTO CHOICE REFORM ACT OF 2001 (H.R.1704) 127

GLOSSARY 151

BIBLIOGRAPHY AND ADDITIONAL RESOURCES 159

ABOUT THE AUTHOR

MARGARET C. JASPER is an attorney engaged in the general practice of law in South Salem, New York, concentrating in the areas of personal injury and entertainment law. Ms. Jasper holds a Juris Doctor degree from Pace University School of Law, White Plains, New York, is a member of the New York and Connecticut bars, and is certified to practice before the United States District Courts for the Southern and Eastern Districts of New York, the United States Court of Appeals for the Second Circuit, and the United States Supreme Court.

Ms. Jasper has been appointed to the panel of arbitrators of the American Arbitration Association and the law guardian panel for the Family Court of the State of New York, is a member of the Association of Trial Lawyers of America, and is a New York State licensed real estate broker and member of the Westchester County Board of Realtors, operating as Jasper Real Estate, in South Salem, New York. Margaret Jasper maintains a website at http://members.aol.com/JasperLaw.

Ms. Jasper is the author and general editor of the following legal almanacs: Juvenile Justice and Children's Law; Marriage and Divorce; Estate Planning; The Law of Contracts; The Law of Dispute Resolution; Law for the Small Business Owner; The Law of Personal Injury; Real Estate Law for the Homeowner and Broker; Everyday Legal Forms; Dictionary of Selected Legal Terms; The Law of Medical Malpractice; The Law of Product Liability; The Law of No-Fault Insurance; The Law of Immigration; The Law of Libel and Slander; The Law of Buying and Selling; Elder Law; The Right to Die; AIDS Law; The Law of Obscenity and Pornography; The Law of Child Custody; The Law of Debt Collection; Consumer Rights Law; Bankruptcy Law for the Individual Debtor; Victim's Rights Law; Animal Rights Law; Workers' Compensation Law; Employee Rights in the Workplace; Probate Law; Environmental Law; Labor Law; The Americans with Disabilities Act; The Law of Capital Punishment; Education Law; The Law of Violence Against Women; Landlord-Tenant Law; Insurance Law; Religion and the Law; Commercial Law; Motor Vehicle Law; Social Security Law; The Law of Drunk Driving; The Law of Speech and the First Amendment; Employment Discrimination Under Title VII; Hospital Liability Law; Home Mortgage Law Primer; Copyright Law; Patent Law; Trademark Law; Special Education Law; The Law of Attachment and Garnishment; Banks and their Customers; and Credit Cards and the Law.

INTRODUCTION

This legal almanac discusses the law of automobile insurance, in general, and focuses on the subcategory of automobile insurance known as "no-fault insurance." Prior to the introduction of no-fault insurance, traditional tort-based liability for damages caused by automobile accidents was the norm. The tort system requires the accident victim to prove that another party was responsible for causing the accident in order to recover damages.

States began to enact no-fault laws as an attempt to reform the manner by which automobile accident victims are compensated. Under this approach, emphasis is placed on compensating the injured without concern for assessing blame. It was hoped that no-fault laws would reduce the number of lawsuits and help to lower the cost of automobile insurance. However, the system proved to have its own shortcomings.

Pure no-fault statutes were never enacted in any jurisdiction. Those which did enact some form of no-fault legislation found that the combined recoveries from the no-fault system and the available tort remedies actually increased automobile insurance premiums. As a result, some states reverted back to their tort-based systems.

Some jurisdictions have attempted to overcome the problems which emanate from both systems by modifying their no-fault system—e.g., by raising the threshold limits which allow a plaintiff to bring a tort action in addition to receiving no-fault benefits.

More recently, the concept of choice-based automobile liability insurance has emerged. The choice-based system permits the purchaser to choose between *no-fault* and *tort-based* coverage.

This almanac sets forth a general discussion of automobile insurance law, with a focus on the history and development of the no-fault system and recent trends. There are variations among the no-fault systems because each jurisdiction's insurance law has evolved largely in response to its own requirements.

For example, requirements as to the minimum liability coverage a driver must maintain may vary according to the jurisdiction's population. A sparsely populated state may not require as much liability insurance.

Thus, readers are cautioned, when researching a particular problem, not to rely on a general discussion of the law, but to always check the law of their own jurisdictions.

The Appendix provides sample documents, applicable statutes, and other pertinent information and data. The Glossary contains definitions of many of the terms used throughout the almanac.

CHAPTER 1:
OVERVIEW OF AUTOMOBILE INSURANCE

THE NATURE OF INSURANCE

Insurance is generally defined as a contract whereby one party, in return for compensation, undertakes to indemnify another party against loss, damages, or liability arising from some contingent or unknown event. The party undertaking the risk is known as the "insurer" or "underwriter." The party who pays for this protection is known as the "insured."

The monies paid by the insured—called "premiums"—are collected from all of the insureds and placed into a general fund from which payments are made to an insured who suffers a covered loss as set forth in the contract. Thus, each insured contributes to some degree for the losses of all of the other insureds. While one insured may never recoup the amount of money paid into the fund, others may be compensated many times over what they have contributed. But that is the nature of insurance—a gamble against the odds.

To this end, the insurer is responsible for calculating premiums that will cover projected losses as well as the administrative and related costs of running the insurance company. The insurer must take into account the number of insureds, the likelihood that the specified losses will occur, and the probable dollar amount of the losses should they occur.

THE ROLE OF THE FEDERAL GOVERNMENT IN INSURANCE LEGISLATION

In 1868, the United States Supreme Court determined in *Paul v. Virginia*, 75 U.S. 168 (1868), that authority to regulate the insurance industry should be left to the individual states, reasoning that insurance contracts were local in nature, and did not affect interstate commerce.

This ruling was reversed in *United States v. South-Eastern Underwriters Association*, 322 U.S. 533 (1944), wherein the Supreme Court held that insurance transactions did affect interstate commerce because, although the contract may be local in nature, the insurance business itself is conducted across state lines, thus implicating the Commerce Clause.

This reversal—in large part due to the expansion of federal powers during the eighty interim years following the *Paul* decision—exposed the insurance industry to federal regulation. Nevertheless, Congress did not intervene and continued to entrust the regulation of the insurance industry to the states by enacting the *McCarran-Ferguson Act* in 1945 which states:

> Congress hereby declares that the continued regulation and taxation by the several States of the business of insurance is in the public interest, and that silence on the part of Congress shall not be construed to impose any barrier to the regulation or taxation of such business by the several States.

Nevertheless, the federal government did retain the right to regulate insurance in cases where (i) a particular state fails to sufficiently regulate a specific activity; or (ii) Congress expressly overrides a state law; or (iii) a state regulation violates the U.S. Constitution.

A Directory of State Insurance Departments is set forth at Appendix 1.

MANDATORY AUTOMOBILE INSURANCE

All states require an individual who registers a car to purchase automobile insurance. Automobile insurance generally protects the insured, the insured's property, and damages sustained to the person and property of individuals as a result of an accident involving the insured. Automobile insurance protects the insured from catastrophic financial losses if they are found to be at fault for an accident. Failure to maintain automobile liability insurance is generally a misdemeanor and subjects the offender to criminal fines and penalties, such as a jail sentence.

A table setting forth the scope of automobile insurance coverage required by each state is set forth at Appendix 2.

THE AUTOMOBILE INSURANCE POLICY

Under an automobile insurance policy, the insured is generally known as the "first party," the insurance carrier is the "second party," and any injured persons are known as "third parties." Elements of coverage common to many automobile insurance policies include: (i) liability coverage; (ii) medical coverage; (iii) collision coverage; (iv) comprehensive coverage; and (v) uninsured motorists coverage, which are discussed further below.

Liability Coverage

Liability coverage indemnifies the insured for the cost of bodily injury and property damage losses sustained by a third party where the insured is determined to be at fault for the accident. Liability limits refer to the dollar amount one's insurance carrier will pay in connection with an accident. The insurance carrier also bears the cost of the insured's legal defense.

Each state sets its own minimum liability insurance requirements. However, although purchasing the minimum would satisfy the legal requirements of the state, individuals with considerable assets should be aware that the state minimums are rarely adequate to cover significant losses, and may expose the insured to additional risk beyond the coverage provided by the policy.

Policy coverage limits are set forth as a series of three numbers, e.g. 50/100/50. The first number refers to the maximum bodily injury coverage per person (e.g., $50,000); the second number refers to the maximum total bodily injury coverage per accident regardless of the number of persons injured (e.g., $100,000); and the third number refers to the upper limit of the insured's property damage protection (e.g., $50,000).

Thus, using the above policy limits, if an accident occurred involving the insured and a third party, where the insured was at fault, the insurance carrier would be liable for up to $50,000 in compensation to each third party for their bodily injuries. One injured person cannot receive more than $50,000 from the insurance carrier regardless of his or her injuries.

Further, if there were five injured persons, the total compensation for all five bodily injury claims cannot exceed a $100,000 payment by the insurance carrier. Thus, the insured would be responsible for the difference between the amounts paid by the insurance carrier, and the damages awarded the injured parties.

In addition, the insurance carrier's property damage exposure is limited to $50,000. Therefore, if the third party's automobile is totalled, and it happens to be worth $75,000, the insured would still be responsible for the difference.

A table of the minimum automobile insurance liability limits required by each state is set forth at Appendix 3.

Medical Coverage

Medical coverage indemnifies the insured for medical expenses incurred by individuals covered under the policy—e.g., the insured and the insured's family. These expenses are known as "first party" expenses. Such expenses may arise as a result of accidents in the insured's vehicle, as well as accidents occurring in other vehicles driven with the owner's permission, and injuries sustained as pedestrians.

Medical expenses are covered regardless of liability, however, the insurance carrier retains the right to recoup such monies from any other party if it is determined that they are at fault for the accident.

Collision Coverage

Collision coverage pays the insured for the cost of damages sustained to the insured's vehicle above the policy deductible. In case of total loss, insurance companies will usually only pay, at a maximum, the "blue book" market value of the vehicle. Collision coverage is usually the most expensive type of insurance coverage, and is not mandatory. Generally, the higher the deductible, the lower the premium. If the insured's vehicle is damaged in an accident, and there is no other party at fault, the insured would have to pay the cost of repairs to the damaged vehicle. Although not mandated by law, collision coverage is generally required by the bank or finance company who leases or finances the vehicle, if applicable.

Comprehensive Coverage

Comprehensive coverage compensates the insured for damages sustained to the car that are not caused by an accident, e.g., fire, theft, vandalism or other natural disaster. Again, in case of total loss, insurance companies will pay, at a maximum, the "blue book" market value of the vehicle. Although not mandated by law, comprehensive coverage is also generally required by the bank or finance company if the automobile is being leased or financed.

Uninsured Motorists Coverage

Uninsured motorists coverage compensates the insured for injuries sustained in accidents with individuals who have no automobile insurance.

Underinsured Motorists Coverage

Underinsured motorists coverage permits the insured to increase liability payments for personal injury and property damage they suffer where the other driver has insufficient coverage.

Supplemental Coverage

Some insurance carriers offer other types of supplemental automobile insurance coverage, including (i) roadside service coverage, e.g., towing and labor expenses; (ii) reimbursement for rental car expenses if the insured's vehicle is stolen or being repaired; and (iii) automobile replacement coverage which guarantees that the vehicle will be repaired or replaced regardless of the blue book value of the car.

Exclusions and Limitations

The automobile policy commonly includes a number of events that are omitted from coverage. These are called exclusions. This may include, for example, damage that was intentionally caused, or caused as the result of drunken driving. It may also specify the limitations on the dollar amounts of coverage you are entitled to receive under the policy. For example, separate limits are generally set for liability, medical payments, uninsured motorists, collision, and comprehensive coverages.

THE COST OF AUTOMOBILE INSURANCE

Insurance rates may vary significantly based upon a number of factors, including but not limited to: (1) the type of car; (2) the driver's record and experience; (3) the driver's age and sex; (4) the driver's place of residence—e.g., areas with high auto theft frequency will generally charge more for comprehensive coverage; and (5) the use of the car, e.g., insurance carriers generally charge a higher rate to individuals who drive their car to and from work.

Prior to issuing a policy, the insurance carrier will generally check with the state's motor vehicle department to determine whether the driver has a clean driving record in order to set the rate.

A Directory of State Motor Vehicle Departments is set forth at Appendix 4.

State insurance departments periodically conduct and publish surveys concerning automobile insurance rates among different insurance companies, and the factors upon which the premiums are based. The reader is advised to check this information as a starting point when shopping around for the best insurance rates.

A table setting forth the average automobile insurance premiums by state is set forth at Appendix 5 and a table setting forth the 10 states with the highest average automobile liability premiums is set forth at Appendix 6.

Because the cost of automobile insurance may vary greatly among different insurance carriers, it is a good idea to comparison shop when purchasing automobile insurance. In addition to shopping around for the best rates, it is important to do some research into the reputation and track record of prospective insurance carriers. Some factors to consider would be the coverage available, and the manner and efficiency in which claims are handled. Information about consumer complaints may be obtained by contacting the state's consumer affairs department and the Better Business Bureau.

A directory of the major casualty and property insurance carriers is set forth at Appendix 7.

Available Discounts

Insurance carriers offer discounts to consumers under certain circumstances, including but not limited to:

1. Drivers with good records, e.g. no accidents or moving violations with a certain period of time.

2. Older drivers, e.g. 55+;

3. Car-pool drivers;

4. Multi-car discounts, e.g., households who insure more than one vehicle with the same insurance carrier;

5. Home/Car Discounts, e.g., insureds who insure both their home and car with the same insurance carrier;

6. Garaged car discounts;

7. Anti-theft device discounts; e.g. Car alarms;

8. Safety device discounts, e.g. air bags; and

9. Safety course completion discounts.

The availability and amount of the particular discount varies, therefore the reader is advised to check with their insurance carrier.

SHARED MARKET INSURANCE PROGRAMS

Some individuals, due to their age, lack of experience, neighborhood, or negative driving record, have difficulty obtaining automobile insurance. Nevertheless, every state has some provision which guarantees such individuals automobile insurance even if an insurance carrier does not wish to provide coverage.

Coverage for drivers who present a considerable risk are usually handled in a pool to which all insurance carriers belong—known as a "shared" market. The insurance premiums may be very high and the coverage not as favorable as policies sold in the "voluntary" market. Approximately 20 percent of all drivers are insured in the "shared market"—also referred to as the "assigned risk" program in some states.

REPORTING THE AUTOMOBILE ACCIDENT

In order to facilitate the processing of the insured's claim through the insurance claims process, following are some guidelines one should consider when involved in an automobile accident.

1. Insist that the police be called to the scene of the accident so that an accurate report of the circumstances surrounding the accident can be recorded. Make sure the police officer takes down your version of the accident.

2. Exchange identification and insurance information with the other driver.

3. Report the accident to your insurance carrier. Your rates will generally not be affected if the accident was not your fault.

4. Review your policy carefully to make sure you understand its provisions and any instructions you must follow in case of an accident. The cover sheet of the policy—also known as the "declarations page"—sets forth the type of coverage and the policy limits. Also review the exclusions section of the policy which sets forth those items your insurance carrier does not cover. If you have any questions, contact your insurance carrier or broker.

If the accident involves property damage, it is important to obtain an estimate from an auto body repair shop. Unfortunately, cars are often declared "totalled"—i.e., a total loss—even though the monetary threshold used in determining the loss—usually market value—is far below the replacement cost of the automobile.

CHAPTER 2:
THE HISTORY AND DEVELOPMENT OF NO-FAULT AUTOMOBILE INSURANCE LAW

TRADITIONAL TORT-BASED LIABILITY SYSTEM

Prior to the introduction of no-fault insurance, traditional tort-based liability was the norm. The tort system requires the accident victim to prove that another party was responsible for causing the accident in order to recover damages. Recovery for personal injuries sustained as a result of an automobile accident was subject to common law negligence rules. This is still the law today in the majority of jurisdictions.

Under this tort-based system, an accident victim recovers damages for both economic and non-economic damages from the party who was responsible for causing the accident and recovers under the bodily injury protection coverage of that party's insurance policy. Such damages include economic losses—e.g., property damage, medical expenses, lost wages; and non-economic damages—e.g. pain and suffering.

Problems with the tort-based system prompted a need for insurance reform. For example, as in any personal injury case, the accident victim must prove the responsible party's negligence in order to prevail—a time consuming process. Contributory and comparative negligence rules also apply which, depending on the jurisdiction, may limit or prevent the plaintiff's recovery. Further, the liability limits of the wrongdoer's liability insurance, if in fact there is insurance, may be so low that it does not fully compensate the accident victim for his or her losses.

INTRODUCTION OF NO-FAULT CONCEPT

In the early 1930s, as automobile ownership increased, a group of Columbia University academicians examined the emerging automobile insurance system and suggested that it be modeled after the workers' compensation system. Benefits would be payable in specific amounts according to a schedule similar to those used in the workers' compensation system.

Proponents of the no-fault system maintained that this new system would ensure an expeditious and full recovery for automobile accident claims without the necessity of litigation. Under their plan, individuals injured in automobile accidents would be compensated by their own insurance company regardless of whether the driver was at fault and non-economic damages such as pain and suffering would be prohibited.

The proposed system was virtually ignored until 1965, when Professors Robert Keeton and Jeffrey O'Connell made revisions to the scheme. They proposed that such a system would be limited to minor auto accidents, under which the injured party would receive compensation for lost wages and medical bills, regardless of fault. Compensation for non-economic damages, would be prohibited in all but the mostserious accidents. Injured individuals who met a monetary threshold of $5,000 would be allowed to litigate their claims in court for non-economic damages and economic costs which exceeded their no-fault benefits.

In the late 1960s and early 1970s, insurance trade associations proposed differing forms of no-fault systems. Large insurance carriers tended to support a "pure" no-fault system which would call for the complete abolition of tort liability in exchange for unlimited medical benefits and substantial wage loss benefits. By 1974, with the considerable resources of the insurance industry in support of the legislation, nineteen states had enacted at least some form of limited no-fault, beginning with Massachusetts in 1971.

The no-fault system was welcomed as a remedy to the inadequacies of the tort system. Proponents of no-fault maintained that the system offered policyholders many benefits, including:

1. The elimination of time-consuming litigation and expensive court costs.

2. More expeditious payment of claims.

3. Elimination of legal fees and fee-splitting.

4. Lower insurance rates making insurance more accessible to lower income drivers.

5. Reduction in the number of lawsuits.

6. No subsidizing uninsured motorists because the medical bills are covered under the policyholder's insurance. covers the cost of your medical bills.

At its peak, twenty-four states had adopted no-fault laws. The laws were hardly uniform, however. Sixteen states instituted a mandatory no-fault system, and eight states enacted hybrid systems in which "no-fault" coverage supplements the required third party liability insurance. Not one state adopted a "pure" no-fault system, which completely bars access to the tort system.

From the mid-1970s through the early 1980s, enactment of no-fault insurance, as well as auto insurance reform in general, was relatively dormant. The District of Columbia is the only state to adopt a no-fault law since 1976. However, automobile insurance reform came to the forefront in the mid-1980's as a result of a liability insurance crisis.

DRAWBACKS OF NO-FAULT SYSTEM

Opponents of no-fault maintained that the system was ineffective and its provisions were unfair, including:

1. No compensation for pain and suffering or other non-economic damages.

2. Protection of bad drivers because they cannot be sued therefore they have no incentive to change their driving habits.

3. Under no-fault, there is a limit even on economic damages whereas under traditional tort systems an injured driver is more fully compensated by suing the responsible driver.

Ironically, the outcome of no-fault, in many cases, increased compensation to accident victims beyond what they would have received under the tort-based system. Benefits were often duplicated and, as a result, insurance premiums skyrocketed. Statistics have shown that rates under no-fault are actually 25% higher on average than in traditional tort liability states. Thus, the expected savings due to a reduction in tort recoveries, which was expected to help finance the no-fault system, did not come to fruition.

A table of states with the highest growth in average auto liability premiums is set forth at Appendix 8.

As a result of these drawbacks, and the unanticipated rise in insurance costs, some jurisdictions which had previously enacted no-fault legislation repealed their no-fault laws due in large part to studies indicating that repeal of the no-fault law would lower the average insurance premium. According to recent statistics, this appears to be the case in those jurisdictions.

A table setting forth the number of no-fault states among the top 10 states with the most expensive automobile insurance rates is set forth at Appendix 9.

Since 1980, six states have repealed their mandatory no-fault laws. Nevada (1980); Georgia (1991); and Connecticut (1994), returned to the personal responsibility system. The District of Columbia moved from mandatory no-fault to an "add-on" system in 1986. New Jersey repealed its mandatory portion of its no-fault law in 1989 as did Pennsylvania in 1990.

CHAPTER 3:
NO-FAULT AUTOMOBILE INSURANCE SCHEMES

NO-FAULT JURISDICTIONS

Presently, there are ten mandatory no-fault jurisdictions: Colorado, Hawaii, Kansas, Massachusetts, Michigan, Minnesota, New York, North Dakota, South Dakota, and Utah. In mandatory no-fault states, lawsuits seeking compensation for pain and suffering are permitted for injuries meeting a certain threshold, the definition of which may vary considerably from state to state.

States with "monetary" thresholds require the victim to demonstrate that their damages exceed a specific dollar amount in order to access the tort system to obtain pain and suffering damages. States with "verbal" thresholds permit such lawsuits only if the injured party can demonstrate a defined level of injury, such as "serious and permanent."

As an example, the text of New York State's verbal threshold for recovery of non-economic damages is set forth at Appendix 10 and a table of state no-fault restrictions on pain and suffering lawsuits is set forth at Appendix 11.

Twelve jurisdictions have hybrid no-fault systems: Arkansas, Delaware, District of Columbia, Kentucky, Maryland, New Jersey, Oregon, Pennsylvania, South Carolina, South Dakota, Texas, and Virginia. In these "add-on" states, there are no limits on lawsuits.

A PURE NO-FAULT SYSTEM

Blame for the rise in insurance costs may be attributed to the fact that, although almost half of all jurisdictions passed some form of no-fault automobile legislation, not one jurisdiction enacted a pure no-fault system. Under a pure no-fault system, accident victims would receive substantial benefits to compensate them for their losses. However, they would have no legal right to pursue a lawsuit against the party responsible for the accident.

The only exceptions in a pure no-fault system would be very narrowly defined, such as those based on public policy grounds—e.g., if the responsible party intended to cause injury, or was driving under the influence of alcohol or drugs.

Opponents of a pure no-fault system argue that it violates the basic tort principle which holds the wrongdoer liable for his or her acts. They reason that no-fault legislation encourages careless driving by eliminating the deterrent effect of a potential lawsuit, and unfairly requires responsible drivers to purchase additional insurance to protect themselves from careless drivers.

Presently, there are no jurisdictions in the United States which have a pure no-fault system. In 1995, a pure no-fault bill was passed by the Hawaii legislature which would have (i) eliminated the accident victim's right to sue for bodily injury; and (ii) established a threshold amount for the right to sue for property damage. However, the bill was vetoed by Governor Cayetano.

FREEDOM OF CHOICE

Freedom of choice refers to the more recent trend toward allowing the customer to decide which type of insurance—no-fault or tort liability—they would like to purchase (the "choice" system). There are variations on the basic options which further define the purchaser's choice, such as the extent to which a tort remedy would be available, e.g. in all instances, or only for certain defined categories of serious injury.

Generally, purchasers who choose to give up their right to maintain tort actions are rewarded with lower premiums, and purchasers who want to retain full rights to bring tort actions pay higher premiums. As further discussed in Chapter 10 of this almanac, Congress introduced the Auto Choice Reform Act in 2001 which would give purchasers of automobile insurance a choice between a no-fault and a tort system of automobile insurance.

Presently, three states offer some type of choice system: Kentucky, New Jersey and Pennsylvania. Pennsylvania's choice system is the most developed to date, as further discussed below.

THE PENNSYLVANIA STATUTE—AN EXAMPLE OF THE CHOICE SYSTEM

In 1990, Pennsylvania became one of the first states to enact choice based automobile liability insurance laws. Under the Pennsylvania statute, insurance companies are obligated to offer customers a choice between limited tort—i.e., no-fault—or full tort insurance.

Under Pennsylvania's limited tort/no-fault option, accident victims recover economic damages from their own insurance carrier, and may sue for non-economic damages under the following circumstances:

1. The responsible party was driving under the influence of drugs or alcohol;

2. The responsible party was operating a motor vehicle registered in another state; and

3. The responsible party intended to cause injury to either himself or another person;

4. The responsible party was driving without legally sufficient insurance, and the accident victim does not have the optional uninsured/underinsured coverage for non-economic loss in his or her own policy.

The Pennsylvania choice system requires the insurer to give the customer written notice, in the policy, of the customer's alternatives under the law. If the customer chooses the limited tort/no-fault option, he or she must sign the notice. If the customer fails to sign the first notice, the insurer is required to send a second notice within 20 days. Failure to sign the second notice serves as forfeiture of the customer's right to elect, and the customer is automatically provided insurance under the full tort-based system.

As no-fault legislation continues to develop, and the insurance industry goes through further reforms in an effort to address the problems inherent in the various alternative systems, the choice system appears to be emerging as a viable option which places the decision in the hands of the consumer.

CHAPTER 4:
COMPONENTS OF THE NO-FAULT INSURANCE SYSTEM

IN GENERAL

No-fault automobile insurance, also known as personal injury protection (PIP), refers to an expanded type of medical coverage required by a number of states and offered by many insurance carriers in states where no-fault is not mandated.

Under the "no-fault" approach, emphasis is placed on compensating the injured without concern for assessing blame. No-fault insurance requires individuals to purchase their own "first party" personal injury protection. If they are injured in an accident, they are able to recover their economic losses—e.g., medical expenses—directly from their own insurance carrier, regardless of who actually caused the accident.

Thus, accident victims do not have to rely on successfully suing the party responsible for the accident in order to receive needed compensation. Nevertheless, under no-fault, the accident victim may be required to give his or her insurance carrier the right of subrogation—i.e., the right to sue the responsible party.

A sample subrogation agreement in a no-fault claim is set forth at Appendix 12.

BASIC ECONOMIC LOSS

Briefly summarized, basic economic loss generally consists of the following benefits up to the jurisdiction's statutorily-prescribed maximum:

1. All necessary doctor and hospital bills and other health service expenses.

2. A percentage of lost earnings.

3. Payment for reasonable and necessary expenses the injured person may have incurred because of an injury resulting from the accident,

such as the cost of hiring a housekeeper or necessary transportation expenses to and from a health service provider.

4. A death benefit payable to the estate of a covered person.

Once the initial coverage for basic economic loss has been exhausted, additional benefits may be available if the applicable insurance policy has been endorsed to include Optional Basic Economic Loss coverage and/or Additional Personal Injury Protection coverage.

No-fault benefits generally continue to be paid until it is determined that the injured person is no longer in need of medical care. Thus, at some point during the period following the motor vehicle accident, the claims representative will set up an appointment with a health care provider to conduct an "independent medical examination." There has been much criticism, however, as to whether or not these examinations are truly "independent," particularly insofar as the independent medical provider is hired by the insurance carrier to conduct the examination and make a determination.

Based upon the results of the medical examination, the claims representative will either continue or deny all or part of the no-fault benefits. Typically, the accident victim's only recourse when faced with a denial of benefits is to appeal to the state's insurance department, or resort to formal arbitration or litigation to have the no-fault benefits reinstated.

LIMITATIONS ON TORT CLAIMS

Although no-fault statutes have been somewhat successful in reducing third party claims, the number of first party claims has necessarily increased, causing premiums to substantially rise. Further, although all no-fault jurisdictions provide some first-party payments for basic economic loss, the reparation schemes are not uniform. Problems still exist in the implementation of the various no-fault schemes, largely because they still permit tort recovery if the accident victim meets certain criteria.

Some jurisdictions permit third party tort claims for damages above the covered basic economic loss, while other jurisdictions place tighter restrictions and limitations on the accident victim's right to pursue third party claims. No jurisdiction has completely banned third party claims. Some jurisdictions tried to limit recoveries by providing that no-fault coverage is merely an "add-on" coverage which cannot be duplicated by tort remedies.

All present no-fault systems permit recourse to the courts against at-fault drivers for payment of economic losses in excess of the no-fault benefits. Further, in all jurisdictions, except Michigan, property damage claims are still subject to the traditional tort system.

Excerpts from Michigan's no-fault insurance statute is set forth at Appendix 13 as an example of a comprehensive no-fault statute.

THE NO-FAULT/TORT LIABILITY SYSTEM

As previously discussed, no jurisdiction has yet enacted pure no-fault legislation. Most jurisdictions which have adopted a no-fault system have also developed a statutory basis for accident victims to maintain a tort action against the responsible party if certain criteria are met.

Under this combined system, the accident victim receives some no-fault economic loss benefits from his or her own insurance carrier regardless of fault. Economic loss refers to medical expenses, lost earnings and expenses for substitute services, such as household help, etc.

Economic damages are readily provable—e.g., by medical bills and employment records, and are thus easy to calculate. However, if the accident victim is reimbursed by a collateral source, such as disability compensation, duplicate benefits would not be permitted for the same expense. Net economic loss represents the accident victim's actual out-of-pocket expenses resulting from the injury.

Under no-fault, first party benefits do not reimburse the accident victim for non-economic damages, such as pain and suffering. However, under the combined system, the accident victims may, under certain defined circumstances, recover non-economic damages in a tort action if they are able to prove that another party caused the accident. Non-economic damages are not as easy to prove and are left to a jury to determine.

A problem which stems from this overlap of systems is the tendency to encourage accident victims to inflate their claims of medical expenses and lost wages so that they meet the threshold which permits them to sue in tort. Because tort recoveries for pain and suffering are often a multiple of the victim's economic loss, he or she may seek additional medical treatment and leave from work. Thus, both the no-fault benefits and tort recoveries for the individual are increased. There is really no incentive for the accident victim to settle for no-fault benefits alone.

In fact, the accident victims in a combined system are able to more comfortably pursue a tort claim because they are receiving first party benefits—e.g., lost wages and medical expenses—from their own insurer, whereas accident victims in traditional tort liability jurisdictions have more of an incentive to settle their claims because they are not receiving any interim financial benefits.

ADD-ON LEGISLATION

Some jurisdictions, in an effort to prevent duplication of benefits, have enacted what is known as "add-on" legislation. In the "add-on" jurisdictions, accident victims are permitted to both (i) receive no-fault benefits; and (ii) pursue a tort action. However, the no-fault benefits cannot be duplicated by the tort recovery, thus, the damages awarded in a tort action would be reduced accordingly.

Presently, the following jurisdictions have enacted "add-on" legislation: Arkansas, Delaware, District of Columbia, Maryland, New Hampshire, Oregon, South Dakota, Texas, Virginia, West Virginia and Wisconsin.

CHAPTER 5:
NO-FAULT COVERAGE ISSUES

IN GENERAL

All no-fault statutes must particularly identify the coverage which is included in its system. This would typically include the type of vehicles covered and their uses, and the persons covered by the insurance. A comprehensive evaluation of each jurisdiction's coverage provisions is not possible in this almanac, therefore, the reader is again cautioned to thoroughly examine the law of their own jurisdiction when researching a particular issue.

COVERED VEHICLES

In general, all private passenger vehicles registered and insured in the particular jurisdiction would be covered under the jurisdiction's no-fault statutes. Generally, motorcycles and mopeds, farm and construction equipment, and government vehicles are excluded from coverage.

An excluded vehicle is usually not required to maintain no-fault insurance. However, this subjects the vehicle's owner to tort actions, and generally prevents injured occupants of the vehicle from receiving any first party benefits. Therefore, following an accident, it is important to first determine whether the vehicle is covered under the jurisdiction's no-fault law.

An accident victim who is not injured in or by a covered vehicle may be disqualified from receiving first party benefits. For example, a pedestrian who is struck by a motorcycle may not be entitled to recover no-fault benefits even if he or she owns a vehicle which has no-fault coverage.

COVERED USES

Covered usage is generally defined as the use, operation or maintenance of the vehicle. In order to recover no-fault benefits, it must be determined that the injuries sustained by the accident victim arose out of such use, operation or maintenance of the vehicle.

Although this may appear simple at first to determine, questions may arise when specific acts are involved, such as when the claimant is injured while entering or leaving the vehicle, or when the claimant is injured while loading groceries into the trunk of the car, or pumping gas. While the law of each jurisdiction may vary according to the facts, entering or leaving a vehicle is generally deemed "occupying" so as to invoke no-fault coverage. However, a slight twist of the facts surrounding the occurrence may make a difference. Nevertheless, the injury must be foreseeably identifiable with the normal use of the vehicle.

For example, a person who is assaulted while stopped at a traffic light may not be entitled to first-party benefits because the assault was not connected with the vehicle, which was merely incidental to the injury.

Exclusions from covered uses may be set forth in the jurisdiction's no-fault statute, or in the insurance contract, and generally include conduct such as: (1) driving while under the influence of alcohol or drugs; (2) driving a stolen vehicle; (3) fleeing from arrest or committing a felony; (4) racing; or (5) any use intended to cause injury to oneself or another.

For example, it has been held that a parked vehicle is not considered a "motor vehicle involved in the accident" and thus not covered, however, a vehicle which is parked in such a way as to cause injury to another motorist may satisfy the "use or maintenance" definition of coverage.

COVERED PERSONS

Most no-fault systems cover: (i) the named insured; (ii) family members of the insured's household; (iii) occupants of the insured vehicle; and (iv) pedestrians who may be injured by the insured vehicle.

A person is generally defined as a family member of the insured's household if he or she is related by blood, marriage or adoption, and lives within the same family unit as the insured. Some courts have extended the definition of "family member" to include persons who live together in a domestic relationship, e.g. unmarried partners and their children, and foster children.

Employees of a corporation may also be entitled to first party benefits. Absent a designation in a corporate vehicle's insurance policy specifically limiting coverage to named employees, the policy would generally cover any employee who is injured while driving the vehicle.

LITIGATION UNDER THE NO-FAULT SYSTEM

The no-fault system was designed to compensate the accident victim in an expedient manner without court involvement. Nevertheless, problems may arise which require legal consultation and, in some cases, litigation. The following scenarios present the most common reasons that no-fault cases proceed to litigation.

First Party Claim

A first party claim arises when the injured party makes a claim for no-fault benefits to his or her insurer, and all or part of the claim is denied or is not timely paid. The accident victim may then seek legal counsel to represent him or her in recovering no-fault benefits.

In such a case, the attorney must determine whether the accident victim is, in fact, entitled to no-fault coverage. If the accident victim is so entitled, the attorney must obtain and evaluate all of the medical records, as well as any official reports and witness statements concerning the accident, in order to support the accident victim's complaint for first party benefits. Some jurisdictions provide for arbitration of no-fault claims.

A sample New York no-fault insurance law arbitration request form is set forth at Appendix 14.

Generally, if a claim cannot be resolved by the arbitration process, a formal lawsuit must be filed to recover no-fault benefits. Many no-fault jurisdictions permit a successful claimant to recover attorney's fees. For example, §3148(1) of Michigan's no-fault statute states:

> An attorney is entitled to a reasonable fee for advising and representing a claimant in an action for personal or property protection insurance benefits which are overdue.

A sample complaint to recover no-fault insurance benefits under New York State law is set forth at Appendix 15.

Third Party Claim

In jurisdictions that allow injured parties to bring a third party claim against the responsible driver, the insurance carrier will scrutinize the medical records of the injured party carefully to make sure they have satisfied the state's no-fault threshold requirements. No-fault thresholds are discussed more fully in Chapter 7 of this almanac.

If the medical records demonstrate that the injured party has not met the state's no-fault threshold, or the issue of liability is in dispute, the insurance carrier will likely deny settling the claim. If an insurance carrier denies settling a case, or makes what appears to be an insignificant offer of settlement, the only recourse is to file a formal lawsuit. However, in cases where it is clear that the client has not meet the no-fault threshold, a lawsuit may not be recommended.

Insurance carriers who do not believe a case has satisfied the no-fault threshold will usually make a motion to the court to dismiss the case for failure to meet the states's requirements. These motions are commonly granted in cases where the monetary threshold has not been met or where a serious injury is difficult to prove and unsupported by medical records.

In addition, a court may award costs and attorney's fees to the defendant or their attorney if it finds that the plaintiff or plaintiff's attorney engaged in frivolous conduct. The court can also impose financial sanctions against the plaintiff or plaintiff's attorney for pursuing a frivolous action, such as one where the no-fault serious injury threshold clearly has not been met.

If the medical records are equivocal—i.e., there is a question as to whether the client has sustained injuries that meet the no-fault threshold—the insurance carrier may also deny settling the case, although most will negotiate in good faith. In offering a settlement under this scenario, the insurance carrier will generally consider such factors as the cost of retaining a lawyer to defend the case and the likelihood that they will be able to have the case dismissed early on in the lawsuit.

Of course, if the medical records indicate that the client has suffered serious injuries which are compensable under the law, it is likely that the insurance carrier will settle the claim. If the insurance carrier refuses to settle a meritorious claim within a reasonable period of time, a formal lawsuit may be commenced.

If an evaluation of the medical records and/or expenses demonstrates that the injured party has satisfied the state's threshold requirements, the attorney may bring a personal injury action against the responsible party. Of course, that party's negligence must be proven in order to recover, and contributory fault rules generally apply.

A sample complaint to recover for personal injury sustained in an automobile accident under New York State law is set forth at Appendix 16.

CHAPTER 6:
FILING THE NO-FAULT APPLICATION

IN GENERAL

Most no-fault systems reimburse accident victims for their basic economic loss, with varying limitations. Such items of reimbursement may include: medical expenses; lost wages; the cost of engaging substitute services, such as a housecleaning service; survivor or death benefits; and funeral and burial expenses. The most commonly paid losses are medical expenses and lost wages.

Following the accident, the insured's insurance carrier provides the accident victim a claims application which must be completed and submitted in order to receive no-fault benefits. A sample application for benefits in connection with a no-fault claim is set forth at Appendix 17.

MEDICAL BENEFITS

Medical benefits generally cover the hospital, doctor and nursing bills. Also covered would be necessary rehabilitation, such as physical therapy. Some jurisdictions place a monetary cap on medical benefits with great variation in the ceiling amount among the jurisdictions. A limit on the time medical benefits may be paid may also apply. Medical expenses generally must be incurred within a certain prescribed time period following the accident.

In making a claim for payment of medical expenses, the accident victim is required to sign authorizations for the release of their medical records from all of the medical providers. A sample authorization form for the release of medical records is set forth at Appendix 18.

The no-fault carrier also requires the medical providers to verify that treatment was undertaken. Sample verification forms for both medical and hospital treatment in connection with a no-fault claim are set forth at Appendix 19 and 20 respectively.

The insurer may also require the accident victim to undergo independent medical examinations—i.e., medical examinations by physicians who are selected by the insurer. A claimant who refuses to submit to these examinations is subject to loss of benefits.

Medical expenses are required to be "reasonable." In order to control the cost of hospital and medical treatment of accident victims, some jurisdictions, such as New York, have set forth a detailed fee schedule which the medical providers must follow.

LOST EARNINGS

No-fault insurance does not provide an accident victim with unlimited reimbursement for lost wages. The various statutory schemes usually compensate victims in one or more of the following methods:

1. Lost wages is one component of the overall no-fault limit, and is not subject to its own monetary ceiling. For example, if the jurisdiction has a no-fault recovery limit of $50,000, lost wages would be computed within that overall figure, along with other items of compensation, such as medical expenses.

2. Lost wages are reimbursed up to a statutory limit, and the accident victim can recover no more than that jurisdiction's limit.

3. Lost wages are subject to a weekly or monthly limit, and the accident victim can recover no more than that jurisdiction's limit per week or month, as applicable.

4. The accident victim may recover only a statutory percentage of gross lost earnings, e.g. eighty percent.

5. Some jurisdictions may set a limit on the time period for which benefits may be paid, e.g. three years.

In making a claim for payment of lost earnings, the accident victim is required to sign an authorization for the release of employment information from their employer. A sample authorization form for the release of employment records is set forth at Appendix 21.

The no-fault carrier also requires the employer to verify the employee's wages. If the accident victim is self-employed, the no-fault carrier requires verification of that income, e.g. by submission of income tax returns. Sample verification forms for both employee wages and self-employment income in connection with a no-fault claim are set forth at Appendix 22 and 23 respectively.

If an accident victim is eligible for disability benefits from a collateral source, e.g. workers compensation or social security disability benefits, etc., the no-fault carrier may require the claimant to pursue such benefits so as not to duplicate compensation. A sample agreement to pursue social security disability benefits in connection with a no-fault claim is set forth at Appendix 24.

SURVIVOR BENEFITS

In the case of a deceased accident victim, no-fault insurance usually does not provide payments to the survivors, who are generally designated as the spouse and children of the decedent. However, benefits may be available to survivors in the form of lost wages of the victim, and payment for substitute services for those that would have been performed by the accident victim. Some jurisdictions pay a flat first-party death benefit to the survivors, who are also permitted to seek further recovery in a wrongful death action against the negligent party.

CHAPTER 7:
TORT ACTION THRESHOLDS

IN GENERAL

Under existing no-fault schemes, a tort recovery is generally still permitted if the accident victim meets certain criteria. In order to recover monetary compensation for "pain and suffering" in a bodily injury claim against the negligent party, the accident victim must satisfy the state's no-fault "threshold."

Bodily injury claims are scrutinized very carefully by insurance carriers to determine whether the no-fault threshold has been reached. Thus, If the medical records clearly indicate that the client has not met the no-fault threshold, or the issue of liability is in dispute, the insurance carrier will most likely deny any monetary settlement.

THE MONETARY THRESHOLD

The dollar threshold permits an accident victim to maintain a lawsuit if their medical expenses exceed a certain minimum dollar amount. There is a broad range of monetary thresholds among the jurisdictions. Some jurisdictions require a very low dollar threshold while others maintain a very high threshold.

For example, New York's no-fault insurance pays medical expenses and lost wages up to a combined total of $50,000. In order to sue in tort, the plaintiff must have sustained economic loss greater than the established ceiling.

THE VERBAL THRESHOLD

The verbal threshold permits an accident victim to maintain a lawsuit if their injuries fall under specified categories of serious injury. Serious injury is usually defined as death, permanent disability, permanent and significant disfigurement, serious fractures, or loss of a body member or function.

Some jurisdictions also have a catch-all category covering accident-related injuries which may not rise to the level of the foregoing serious injuries. Under this category, the accident victim must have been disabled for a prescribed period of time following the accident, e.g. 90 days out of the first 180 days following the accident.

For example, New York State's no-fault law defines a "serious injury" as "a personal injury which results in:

1. Death;

2. Dismemberment;

3. Significant disfigurement;

4. A fracture;

5. Loss of a fetus;

6. Permanent loss of use of a body organ or member;

7. Significant limitation of use of a body organ or member;

8. Significant limitation of use of a body function or system; or

9. A medically determined injury or impairment of a non-permanent nature which prevents the plaintiff from performing substantially all of the material acts which constitute plaintiff's usual and customary daily activities for not less than ninety days during the one hundred-eighty days immediately following the occurrence of the injury or impairment."

Jurisdictions which have enacted threshold requirements include Colorado, Florida, Hawaii, Kansas, Kentucky, Massachusetts, Michigan, Minnesota, New Jersey, New York, North Dakota, Pennsylvania, and Utah.

Out-Of-Balance No-Fault Laws

A major problem with no-fault legislation exists in jurisdictions which have low thresholds. According to the Department of Transportation, such jurisdictions are known as having an "out-of-balance" no-fault law. This is due to the fact that such jurisdictions often allow victims unlimited medical benefits and substantial lost wage benefits while also permitting tort claims if the medical losses exceed a low dollar threshold. For example, Colorado's monetary threshold is only $2,500. Because this low monetary threshold is easily met, plaintiffs are almost always able to recover no-fault compensation as well as sue in tort.

New York is one jurisdiction which has experienced moderate success with its no-fault system, and which would be considered an "in-balance" jurisdiction according to the Department of Transportation. This is due to the fact that it maintains a higher no-fault threshold which must be met before it allows a plaintiff to sue in tort.

New York's monetary threshold is $50,000 and, as set forth above, New York's verbal threshold requires a significant injury to maintain an action in tort. The language of the New York statute is set forth at Appendix 10 as an example of an "in-balance" no-fault statute.

If an accident victim pursues a tort action, the facts which meet the verbal or economic threshold and take the case out of no-fault must be set forth in the complaint. Again, refer to the language of the sample complaint to recover for personal injury sustained in an automobile accident under New York State law which is set forth at Appendix 16.

CHAPTER 8:
CHOICE OF LAW ISSUES

IN GENERAL

When two jurisdictions have an interest in the outcome of a controversy, and their applicable law is diverse, the court in which the action is pending must decide which jurisdiction's law should apply to the controversy. This is referred to as "choice of law" or "conflict of law".

Because some jurisdictions have enacted no-fault legislation, while other jurisdictions have chosen to retain tort-based recovery systems, choice of law problems may arise when a driver from a no-fault jurisdiction has an accident with a driver from a tort-based jurisdiction. This problem may also occur within a particular state that chooses the "freedom of choice" insurance system.

Under Michigan's no-fault statute, benefits are payable for accidental bodily injury suffered in an accident occurring out of state if: (1) the accident occurs within the United States, its territories and possessions or in Canada; and (2) the person whose injury is the basis of the claim was at the time of the accident: (a) a named insured under a personal protection insurance policy; or (b) had a spouse or a relative domiciled in the same household who was insured under a personal protection insurance policy; or (c) an occupant of a vehicle involved in the accident whose owner or registrant was insured under a personal protection insurance policy.

Excerpts from Michigan's no-fault statute are set forth at Appendix 13.

Nevertheless, most jurisdictions did not include statutory methods of resolving such conflict of law situations in their no-fault legislation. The case law which necessarily followed developed three tests to resolve the conflict: (1) The Most Significant Relationship Test; (2) Lex Loci Contractus; and (3) Lex Loci Delecti.

THE MOST SIGNIFICANT RELATIONSHIP TEST

The Restatement of Conflict of Laws, Second, states that the law of the jurisdiction which has the most significant relationship to the controversy should apply, taking into account factors such as the site of the injury, the domiciles of the parties, and the place of contract, etc. The most significant relationship test appears to be emerging as the favored method of resolving the conflict.

LEX LOCI CONTRACTUS

Lex Loci Contractus is an ancient legal concept in contract law which basically states that the law of the place where the contract was made will be determinative in a conflict of law situation. Many jurisdictions have applied this concept to automobile accident litigation and have applied the law of the place where the insurance contract was made, while other jurisdictions use the place of contract as just another factor to be considered in the significant relationship choice of law method.

LEX LOCI DELECTI

Lex Loci Delecti refers to the application of the law where the wrong occurred to resolve a controversy. Although this concept has been applied in automobile accident cases, it is primarily used as yet another factor to be considered in the significant relationship choice of law method.

Until statutes are enacted to address the various conflict of law situations which may arise as a result of the diversity of insurance systems, the courts will continue to struggle with the proper method of fairly resolving such conflicts.

CHAPTER 9:
NO-FAULT AUTOMOBILE INSURANCE FRAUD

IN GENERAL

As discussed earlier, the purpose of the no-fault auto insurance system was to lower insurance costs by limiting the number of small claims that proceed to litigation. Under no-fault, the insurance company compensates its own insureds for economic losses, including medical costs, regardless of who was at fault for the accident ("first party benefits"). Specific provisions of the "first party" benefits vary from state to state.

According to the FBI, there is a growing problem of no-fault automobile insurance fraud, which is due, in large part, to criminal schemes involving organized crime rings. Along with unethical medical providers and lawyers, they manipulate the personal injury protection feature of the no-fault system at the financial expense of legitimate policyholders.

THE NATURE OF NO-FAULT INSURANCE FRAUD

Automobile insurance fraud includes acts such as staging an accident, filing a fraudulent police report and filing false medical claims. Unscrupulous medical clinics pay individuals—commonly referred to as "runners"—to arrange simple auto accidents and recruit passengers. They then send purportedly "injured" persons to the medical clinic for treatment.

These staged accidents are minor and are not intended to cause serious injuries to the drivers or passengers. However, they are reported to the police so that a police report can be generated to support the fraudulent insurance claim. In addition, the "injured" person generally requests that an ambulance be called so that an ambulance report may also be generated and lend further credibility to the claim.

The runners then direct the "injured" to the medical clinic for unnecessary medical treatment and the clinic submits claims under the insurance policy of the runner or other person who insured the car. A single staged accident with a number of "injured" passengers is quite lucrative for medical clinics.

In addition to the medical costs generated, attorneys involved in the scheme file bodily injury claims on behalf of the "injured" party based on the inflated medical records. These claims are usually settled to avoid litigation. An insurance carrier will often offer "nuisance value" even when there is a question as to whether the injuries sustained meet the state's no-fault threshold. Nuisance value alone can range from $2,500 to $5,000 per claimant.

Thus, there is a built-in incentive for claimants to exaggerate their claims in order to establish a basis to bring a bodily injury lawsuit in court. In order to combat this scheme, some insurance companies have begun to deny settling questionable claims and force the attorney to file a formal action, which is more costly. The insurance carrier will then make a motion to the court to dismiss the action on the basis that it does not meet the necessary threshold for recovery of non-economic damages.

TYPES OF FRAUDULENT PRACTICES

Some of the fraudulent practices carried out under no-fault insurance scams include:

Fraudulent Billing Practices

Medical clinics involved in no-fault insurance fraud often bill the insurance carrier for services not rendered to the insured. In the most extreme cases, investigations have found that the medical clinic does not exist and the so-called medical provider was simply billing the insurance carrier for nonexistent patients. To try and combat this practice, insurance companies conduct independent medical evaluations of the injured parties to verify their injuries.

Insurance carriers also receive bills for medical supplies that were never supplied to the insured and transportation expenses which were never incurred. It was also found that some doctors and lawyers actually own a share of the transportation companies that are used to transport claimants to certain clinics. These costs often exceed thousands of dollars. In a number of cases, the insured is not even aware that these fraudulent bills have been generated.

Another fraudulent practice is to bill for an excessive use of all types of non-traditional medical treatment, such as acupuncture, aromatherapy, and biofeedback, etc. These treatments often require numerous visits which greatly inflate the medical costs.

False Claims of Household Help

Where an insured is entitled to reimbursement for necessary expenses resulting from the accident, such as household help, they have submitted claims falsely stating they have had to hire household help when, in fact, they have not had any such assistance, or they have submitted false documentation as to the hours worked.

False Lost Wages Claims

Where an insured is entitled to lost wages under their state's no-fault system, many unemployed insureds have falsely claimed lost wages and supplied false or forged documents to substantiate their claims.

Multiple Claims—Identity Fraud

A claimant in a no-fault insurance fraud case generally fakes both the accident and their injuries. However, they often do so under stolen identities in order to protect their own identity. In this way, they can make multiple claims under a variety of assumed identities at the same time.

REFORM MEASURES

A number of legislative and regulatory measures have been explored to try and combat the problem of automobile insurance fraud while still protecting the rights of legitimate policyholders and medical providers. Some suggested reforms include making it illegal to act as a middleman between a claimant and a medical provider, thus subjecting "runners" to criminal prosecution; a requirement that a no-fault insurer receive notice within five days of treatment from a medical provider for an assignment of benefits to be valid thus allowing the insurer to contain the costs at inception rather than being confronted much later with excessive billing for unnecessary procedures already performed; precertification requirements for certain medical procedures; and mandatory no-fault arbitration procedures.

NO-FAULT INSURANCE FRAUD IN NEW YORK

New York is the state that has been hardest hit by automobile insurance fraud schemes. New York's no-fault auto insurance law became effective in 1974. In New York, first party benefits include medical costs, lost wages, funeral costs and other out-of-pocket expenses resulting from an accident. New York's no-fault system also restricts the injured party's right to sue for non-economic damages, e.g., pain and suffering, unless the cost of the insured's claim exceeds $50,000 or the insured's injuries meet the verbal threshold.

In 1999, medical no-fault claim costs in New York rose by almost one-third. Claims costs in New York rose by 11.1% as compared to a 4.5% increase in 1998. This increase is due to the fact that there are more claims being filed as well as a large increase in the average cost per claim.

According to law enforcement, both cost increases are almost entirely fraud-driven. The rise in frequency and cost of medical no-fault claims cannot be explained by any economic factors such as increases in medical inflation because medical professionals under the no-fault law in New York State are paid according to a fee schedule which fixes the price for medical goods and services.

According to the Insurance Fraud Bureau, no-fault fraud reports now account for 55% of all reported insurance frauds. The National Insurance Crime Bureau reports that last year, 90% of its fraud referrals in New York involved auto insurance fraud.

The financial impact of this rise in insurance fraud has caused insurance rates in New York to skyrocket. Insurance companies pay almost twice as much in personal injury protection costs as they receive in premiums. It is estimated that no-fault fraud will cost insurance companies doing business in New York State and their policyholders one billion dollars this year alone. Insurance carriers spend millions of dollars to hire investigators to root out no-fault fraud in New York. However, they maintain that an overall reform of the system is necessary to help control the fraud.

One measure that was passed in 1994 permits insurance carriers to offer their insureds the opportunity to get a discount on their personal injury protection—i.e., no-fault—coverage. However, to be eligible for the discount, the insured must agree to go to a health care provider associated with a managed care organization (MCO) designated by the insurance carrier if injured in an auto accident. This would allow the carrier to maintain stricter controls over the insured's medical treatment plan. The carrier must provide the insured with a list of medical providers who participate in the managed care option prior to that person agreeing to the option and, in the event the insured is ever injured, the managed care option is supposed to provide any and all of the health care services which would otherwise be available to the injured party if he had not selected the managed care option.

Generally, when an individual is injured in an auto accident, they may go to the medical provider of their own choice, provided that the provider "takes no-fault cases"—i.e., agrees to bill according to the no-fault fee schedule. The injured party and the medical provider determine the type of care and any testing necessary to diagnose and treat the injury.

However, if an injured party who has opted for the managed care option goes to a medical provider who is not a participant in the managed care option, the patient is deemed to be "opting out," and would be subject to a considerable penalty, which may consist of a deductible up to $2,500 and/or a co-payment of up to 25 percent.

CHAPTER 10:
AUTO CHOICE REFORM ACT OF 2001

OVERVIEW

Federal legislation is presently pending in the House of Representatives which would change automobile insurance coverage nationwide. Based on its findings, Congress has blamed the tort liability insurance system for, among other things: (1) excessive insurance rates; (2) failure to provide compensation commensurate with loss; (3) unreasonable delay in payment of losses; (4) excessive legal fees; (5) fraud in the claims process; and (6) fraud and abuse of health care resources.

In an effort to curb these abuses, and ultimately bring down the costs of automobile insurance, Rep. Richard Armey (R-Texas) introduced the Auto Choice Reform Act of 2001 (H.R. 1704). The bill's stated purpose is "to enable drivers to choose a more affordable form of auto insurance that also provides for more adequate and timely compensation for accident victims."

The Act would give purchasers of automobile insurance a choice—not a mandate—between two insurance systems: (1) The Personal Injury Protection System; and (2) The Tort Maintenance System. Those who fail to select a type of insurance will be deemed to have elected insurance under the tort maintenance system.

The Act does not propose to abolish the right to sue nor eliminate the concept of fault within the legal system. However, it does allow drivers to decide how they want to be insured. In particular, as discussed below, drivers would have the option to remain with traditional tort liability coverage and could decide whether they wanted to pay a significant portion of their premium for the expensive and often protracted alternative of suing for noneconomic damages. Consumers who elect to opt out of the "pain and suffering" litigation pool would be rewarded with substantial savings on automobile insurance premiums.

The full text of the Auto Choice Reform Act of 2001 is set forth at Appendix 25.

REDUCTION IN INSURANCE PREMIUMS

Supporters of the bill maintain that it would give drivers the opportunity to reduce their auto insurance premiums by an average of 26%. They contend that this would be particularly significant in poor urban neighborhoods where, according to the U.S. Department of Labor, families in the bottom 20 percent of income spend seven times the percentage of their household earnings on auto insurance as do families in the top 20 percent. It would also impact middle-income families, who spend on average 150% more on auto insurance than they do on education.

Increasing the affordability of auto insurance will also help to reduce the growing problem of uninsured drivers. According to a Congressional Joint Economic Committee report, there is a direct and substantial relationship between the cost of auto insurance and the percentage of drivers who obtain coverage. For example, a 40% reduction in auto insurance premiums would likely result in a 50% reduction in the number of uninsured drivers.

REDUCTION IN FRAUDULENT CLAIMS

The Act is also intended to reduce the growing problem of insurance fraud which, according to the FBI, costs every American an average of $200 dollars a year. The Act seeks to protect against insurance fraud by limiting the payment of first party benefits to personal injury protection claimants to 60 days following submission of claims.

Insurers will not be obligated to pay first party benefits to personal injury protection insureds should a court determine that the claims are, in whole or in part, the product of fraudulent activities by the insureds. This in turn will allow the majority of people to be more fully and expeditiously compensated, and to receive a fairer return on their auto insurance investment, under the personal protection insurance option.

The Act also allows insurers to cancel, decline to renew, or refuse to issue a personal injury protection policy to those who have been convicted of fraudulent activities, with respect to accidents, during the three years prior to application.

THE TORT MAINTENANCE SYSTEM

Under the Act, a driver who wishes to retain the right to sue for non-economic damages can do so by choosing traditional tort liability coverage. The only difference is that the injured party, after proving fault or negligence, would be compensated by his or her own insurance company for the non-economic damages.

The driver would essentially buy the same type of insurance that they currently carry—and would recover, or fail to recover, in the same way that they currently do. The only change for tort drivers would be that, in the event that they are hit by a personal protection driver, the tort driver would recover both economic and noneconomic damages from his or her own insurance policy. This supplemental first-party policy for tort drivers is called tort maintenance coverage.

THE PERSONAL INJURY PROTECTION SYSTEM

If a driver wants to opt-out of pain and suffering coverage, he or she chooses the personal injury protection system. The personal injury protection option allows a driver to be compensated by his or her own insurance company without proving fault. Under this option, drivers may sue for lost wages and medical costs above their policy limits, but not for pain and suffering except in cases where a drunk driver, drug abuse or intentional endangerment injured an insured.

Drivers choosing this system would be guaranteed prompt recovery of their economic losses, up to the levels of their own insurance policy. These drivers would give up recovery of pain and suffering damages in exchange for immunity from pain and suffering lawsuits. Personal injury protection drivers would achieve substantially reduced premiums because the personal injury protection system would dramatically reduce pain and suffering damages; fraud; and most attorney fees.

Nevertheless, under both insurance systems, the injured party whose economic losses exceed his own coverage will have the right to sue the responsible party for the excess. Moreover, tort maintenance system drivers will retain the right to sue each other for both economic and noneconomic loss.

CONSUMER NOTIFICATION PROGRAM

The Act authorizes the appropriate state official to establish a consumer notification program regarding: (1) the comparative cost of insurance under the personal injury protection and tort maintenance systems; and (2) the benefits, rights, and obligations of the insurers and insureds under each system. The Act also requires insurers to provide this information to a consumer before the consumer chooses insurance.

STATE REGULATION

The Act would also leave regulation of insurance to the states and would exempt a state from application of the Act if the state: (1) declares by statute by a specified date that this Act shall not apply; or (2) finds that average premiums will not be reduced by an average of at least 30 percent for persons choosing the personal injury protection system.

Further, each state would be able to retain the best elements of their current system. Bad drivers would still be punished with higher premiums; injured parties would still be able to sue a negligent driver for economic damages in excess of the plaintiff's coverage; and an insured driver would still be able to seek compensation from his own carrier if he is involved in an accident with an uninsured driver.

APPENDIX 1:
DIRECTORY OF STATE INSURANCE DEPARTMENTS

STATE	DEPARTMENT	ADDRESS	TELEPHONE NUMBER
Alabama	Department of Insurance	201 Monroe Street, Suite 1700, Montgomery, Alabama 36104	205-269-3550
Alaska	Division of Insurance	State Office Building, 333 Willoughby Avenue, 9th Floor, P.O. Box 110805, Juneau, Alaska 99811-0805	907-465-2515
Arizona	Department of Insurance	2910 N. 44th Street, Suite 210, Phoenix, Arizona 85018	602-255-5400
Arkansas	Department of Insurance	1200 West 3rd Street, Little Rock, Arkansas 72201-1904	501-686-2900
California	Department of Insurance	300 Capital Mall, Suite 1500, Sacramento, California 95814	800-927-4357
Colorado	Division of Insurance	1560 Broadway, Suite 850, Denver, Colorado 80202	303-894-7499
Connecticut	Insurance Department	P.O. Box 816, Hartford, Connecticut 06142-0816	860-297-3802

STATE	DEPARTMENT	ADDRESS	TELEPHONE NUMBER
Delaware	Department of Insurance	1st Federal Plaza, 710 North King Street, Wilmington, Delaware 19801	800-282-8611
District of Columbia	Department of Insurance	441 Fourth St. NW, 8th Floor North, Washington, DC 20001	202-727-8002
Florida	Department of Insurance	9000 Regency Square Boulevard, Suite 201, Jacksonville, Florida 32211	800-342-2762
Georgia	Office of Commissioner of Insurance	2 Martin Luther King, Jr. Drive, Atlanta, Georgia 30334	404-656-2056
Hawaii	Insurance Commissioner's Office	250 S. King Street, Honolulu, Hawaii 96813	800-468-4644
Idaho	Department of Insurance	700 West State Street, Boise, Idaho 83720-0043	208-334-2250
Illinois	Department of Insurance	320 West Washington Street, 4th Floor, Springfield, Illinois 62767	217-782-4515
Indiana	Department of Insurance	311 West Washington Street, Suite 300, Indianapolis, Indiana 46204-2787	800-622-4461
Iowa	Insurance Division	Lucas Building, 6th Floor, Des Moines, Iowa 50319	515-281-5705
Kansas	Insurance Department	420 S.W. Ninth Street, Topeka, Kansas 66612-1678	800-432-2484
Kentucky	Department of Insurance	215 West Main Street, Frankfort, Kentucky 40601	502-564-3630
Louisiana	Department of Insurance	950 North Fifth Street, Baton Rouge, Louisiana 70804-9214	504-342-5900
Maine	Bureau of Insurance	34 State House Station, Augusta, Maine 04333	207-582-8707

STATE	DEPARTMENT	ADDRESS	TELEPHONE NUMBER
Maryland	Insurance Administration	525 St. Paul Place, Baltimore, Maryland 21202	800-492-6116
Massachusetts	Division of Insurance	470 Atlantic Avenue, 6th Floor, Boston, Massachusetts 02110-2223	617-727-3357
Michigan	Insurance Bureau	611 West Ottawa Street, 2nd Floor North, Lansing, Michigan 48933	517-373-9273
Minnesota	Division of Insurance	133 East 7th Street, St. Paul, Minnesota 55101	800-652-9747
Mississippi	Department of Insurance	1804 Walter Sillers Building, Jackson, Mississippi 39201	601-359-3569
Missouri	Department of Insurance	P.O. Box 690, Jefferson City, Missouri 65102-0690	314-751-4126
Montana	Department of Insurance	126 North Sanders, Room 270, Helena, Montana 59620	800-332-6148
Nebraska	Department of Insurance	941 O Street, Suite 400, Lincoln, Nebraska 68508-3690	402-471-2201
Nevada	Department of Insurance	1665 Hot Springs Road, Suite 152, Carson City, Nevada 89710	800-992-0900
New Hampshire	Insurance Department	169 Manchester Street, Suite 1, Concord, New Hampshire 03301-5151	800-852-3416
New Jersey	Department of Insurance	20 West State Street, CN325, Trenton, New Jersey 08625-0325	609-292-5363
New Mexico	Insurance Division	P.O. Drawer 1269, Santa Fe, New Mexico 87504-1269	505-827-4500

STATE	DEPARTMENT	ADDRESS	TELEPHONE NUMBER
New York	Insurance Department	Empire State Plaza, Agency Building No. 1, Albany, New York 12257	518-474-6600
North Carolina	Department of Insurance	P.O. Box 26387, Raleigh, North Carolina 27611	800-662-7777
North Dakota	Department of Insurance	600 East Boulevard, Bismarck, North Dakota 58505-0320	800-247-0560
Ohio	Department of Insurance	2100 Stella Court, Columbus, Ohio 43215-1067	800-686-1526
Oklahoma	Department of Insurance	3814 N. Santa Fe, Oklahoma City, Oklahoma 73118	405-521-1828
Oregon	Insurance Division	350 Winter St. NE, Room 200, Salem, Oregon 97310-0200	503-378-4271
Pennsylvania	Department of Insurance	1326 Strawberry Square, Harrisburg, Pennsylvania 17120	717-787-5173
Rhode Island	Insurance Department	233 Richmond Street, Suite 233, Providence, Rhode Island 02903-4233	401-277-2223
South Carolina	Department of Insurance	P.O. Box 100105, Columbia, South Carolina 29202-3105	803-737-6117
South Dakota	Insurance Division	500 East Capitol, Pierre, South Dakota 57501-5070	605-773-3563
Tennessee	Department of Insurance	500 James Robertson Parkway, Nashville, Tennessee 37243-0565	800-342-4029
Texas	Department of Insurance	P.O. Box 149104, Austin, Texas 78714-9104	512-463-6464

STATE	DEPARTMENT	ADDRESS	TELEPHONE NUMBER
Utah	Insurance Department	3110 State Office Building, Salt Lake City, Utah 84114	801-530-6400
Vermont	Insurance Division	89 Main Street, Drawer 20, Montpelier, Vermont 05620-3101	802-828-3301
Virginia	Bureau of Insurance	P.O. Box 1157, Richmond, Virginia 23218	800-552-7945
Washington	Office of Insurance Commissioner	P.O. Box 40255, Olympia, Washington 98504-0255	800-562-6900
West Virginia	Insurance Department	P.O. Box 50540, Charleston, West Virginia 25305-0540	800-642-9004
Wisconsin	Office of the Commissioner of Insurance	121 East Wilson Street, Madison, Wisconsin 53702	800-236-8517
Wyoming	Insurance Department	122 West 25th Street, 3rd Floor East, Cheyenne, Wyoming 82002-0440	307-777-7401

Source: Insurance Information Institute.

APPENDIX 2:
SCOPE OF AUTOMOBILE INSURANCE
COVERAGE REQUIRED BY EACH STATE

STATE	TYPE OF COVERAGE REQUIRED
Alabama	Bodily Injury and Property Damage Liability
Alaska	Bodily Injury and Property Damage Liability
Arizona	Bodily Injury and Property Damage Liability
Arkansas	Bodily Injury and Property Damage Liability
California	Bodily Injury and Property Damage Liability, Personal Injury Protection
Colorado	Bodily Injury and Property Damage Liability, Personal Injury Protection
Connecticut	Bodily Injury and Property Damage Liability, Uninsured and Underinsured Motorist
Delaware	Bodily Injury and Property Damage Liability, Personal Injury Protection
D.C.	Bodily Injury and Property Damage Liability, Uninsured Motorist
Florida	Property Damage Liability, Personal Injury Protection
Georgia	Bodily Injury and Property Damage Liability
Hawaii	Bodily Injury and Property Damage Liability, Personal Injury Protection
Idaho	Bodily Injury and Property Damage Liability
Illinois	Bodily Injury and Property Damage Liability, Uninsured Motorist
Indiana	Bodily Injury and Property Damage Liability
Iowa	Bodily Injury and Property Damage Liability

STATE	TYPE OF COVERAGE REQUIRED
Kansas	Bodily Injury and Property Damage Liability, Personal Injury Protection, Uninsured Motorist
Kentucky	Bodily Injury and Property Damage Liability, Personal Injury Protection
Louisiana	Bodily Injury and Property Damage Liability
Maine	Bodily Injury and Property Damage Liability, Uninsured Motorist
Maryland	Bodily Injury and Property Damage Liability, Personal Injury Protection (may be waived for policyholder but compulsory for passengers), Uninsured Motorist
Massachusetts	Bodily Injury and Property Damage Liability, Personal Injury Protection, Uninsured Motorist
Michigan	Bodily Injury and Property Damage Liability, Personal Injury Protection
Minnesota	Bodily Injury and Property Damage Liability, Personal Injury Protection, Uninsured and Underinsured Motorist
Mississippi	Financial Responsibility Only
Missouri	Bodily Injury and Property Damage Liability, Underinsured Motorist
Montana	Bodily Injury and Property Damage Liability
Nebraska	Bodily Injury and Property Damage Liability
Nevada	Bodily Injury and Property Damage Liability
New Hampshire	Financial Responsibility Only
New Jersey	Bodily Injury and Property Damage Liability, Personal Injury Protection, Uninsured Motorist
New Mexico	Bodily Injury and Property Damage Liability
New York	Bodily Injury and Property Damage Liability, Personal Injury Protection, Uninsured Motorist
North Carolina	Bodily Injury and Property Damage Liability
North Dakota	Bodily Injury and Property Damage Liability, Personal Injury Protection, Uninsured Motorist
Ohio	Bodily Injury and Property Damage Liability
Oklahoma	Bodily Injury and Property Damage Liability

STATE	TYPE OF COVERAGE REQUIRED
Oregon	Bodily Injury and Property Damage Liability, Personal Injury Protection, Uninsured Motorist
Pennsylvania	Bodily Injury and Property Damage Liability, Medical Payments
Rhode Island	Bodily Injury and Property Damage Liability, Uninsured Motorist
South Carolina	Bodily Injury and Property Damage Liability, Uninsured Motorist
South Dakota	Bodily Injury and Property Damage Liability, Uninsured Motorist
Tennessee	Financial Responsibility Only
Texas	Bodily Injury and Property Damage Liability
Utah	Bodily Injury and Property Damage Liability, Personal Injury Protection
Vermont	Bodily Injury and Property Damage Liability, Uninsured and Underinsured Motorist
Virginia	Bodily Injury and Property Damage Liability, Uninsured Motorist
Washington	Bodily Injury and Property Damage Liability
West Virginia	Bodily Injury and Property Damage Liability, Uninsured Motorist
Wisconsin	Financial Responsibility Only, Uninsured Motorist
Wyoming	Bodily Injury and Property Damage Liability

APPENDIX 3:
STATE AUTOMOBILE INSURANCE
MINIMUM MONETARY LIABILITY CHART

STATE	AMOUNT (In Thousands of Dollars)
Alabama	20/40/10
Alaska	50/100/25
Arizona	15/30/10
Arkansas	25/50/15
California	15/30/5
Colorado	25/50/15
Connecticut	20/40/10
Delaware	15/30/5
D.C.	25/50/10
Florida	10/20/10
Georgia	15/30/10
Hawaii	20/40/10
Idaho	25/50/15
Illinois	20/40/15
Indiana	25/50/10
Iowa	20/40/15
Kansas	25/50/10
Kentucky	25/50/10
Louisiana	10/20/10
Maine	50/100/25

STATE	AMOUNT (In Thousands of Dollars)
Maryland	20/40/10
Massachusetts	20/40/5
Michigan	20/40/10
Minnesota	30/60/10
Mississippi	10/20/5
Missouri	25/50/10
Montana	25/50/10
Nebraska	25/50/25
Nevada	15/30/10
New Hampshire	25/50/25
New Jersey	15/30/5
New Mexico	25/50/10
New York	25/50/10*
North Carolina	25/50/15
North Dakota	25/50/25
Ohio	12.5/25/7.5
Oklahoma	10/20/10
Oregon	25/50/10
Pennsylvania	15/30/5
Rhode Island	25/50/25
South Carolina	15/30/10
South Dakota	25/50/25
Tennessee	20/50/10
Texas	20/40/15
Utah	25/50/15
Vermont	25/50/10
Virginia	25/50/20
Washington	25/50/10
West Virginia	20/40/10

STATE	AMOUNT (In Thousands of Dollars)
Wisconsin	25/50/10
Wyoming	25/50/20

Note: The first number denotes the bodily injury liability maximum for one person injured in an accident; the second number denotes the bodily injury maximum for all injuries in one accident; the third number denotes the property damage liability maximum for one accident;

* liability raised to 50/100 if death occurs.

APPENDIX 4:
DIRECTORY OF STATE MOTOR VEHICLE DEPARTMENTS

STATE	AGENCY	ADDRESS	TELEPHONE
ALABAMA	Department of Public Safety, Driver License Records Unit	P.O. Box 1471, Montgomery, AL 36192-2301	(205) 242-4400
ALASKA	Department of Public Safety, Division of Motor Vehicles Driver Services	P.O. Box 20020, Juneau, AK 99802-0020	(907) 465-4335
ARIZONA	Motor Vehicle Division, Office of Driver Improvement	P.O. Box 2100, Phoenix, AZ 85001	(602) 255-0072
ARKANSAS	Office of Driver Services, Driver Control Section	P.O. Box 1272, Little Rock, AR 72203	(501) 682-1400
CALIFORNIA	Department of Motor Vehicles, Driver License Operations	P.O. Box 942890, Sacramento, CA 94290-0001	(916) 657-6525
COLORADO	Motor Vehicle Division, Driver Control Section	140 West 6th Avenue, Denver, CO 80204	(303) 205-5613
CONNECTICUT	Department of Motor Vehicles, Driver Services Division	60 State Street, Wethersfield, CT 06109	(860) 566-5250

STATE	AGENCY	ADDRESS	TELEPHONE
DELAWARE	Division of Motor Vehicles, Driver Improvement Section	P.O. Box 698, Dover, DE 19903	(302) 739-4497
DISTRICT OF COLUMBIA	Bureau of Motor Vehicle Services, Traffic Records and Rehab Branch,	301 C Street NW, Washington, DC 20001	(202) 727-6761
FLORIDA	Bureau of Records	P.O. Box 5775, Tallahassee, FL 32314-5775	(904) 488-9145
GEORGIA	Department of Public Safety, Revocation Section	P.O. Box 1456, Atlanta, GA 30371	(404) 624-7561
HAWAII	Motor Vehicle Safety Office	1505 Dillingham Blvd., Suite 214, Honolulu, HI 96817	(808) 832-5826
IDAHO	Motor Vehicle Bureau, Driver Services Section	P.O. Box 7129, Boise, ID 83707	(208) 334-8736
ILLINOIS	Department of Motor Vehicles, Driver Services Division	2701 South Dirksen Parkway, Springfield, IL 62723	(217) 785-1687
INDIANA	Bureau of Motor Vehicles, Safety Responsibility & Driver Improvement	State Office Building, Room 410, Indianapolis, IN 46204	(317) 232-2894
IOWA	Driver Records	100 Euclid, Park Fair Mall, P.O. Box 9204, Des Moines, IA 50306-9204	(515) 244-9124
KANSAS	Division of Vehicles, Driver Control & Licensing Bureau	Robert Docking State Office Building, Topeka, KS 66626	(913) 296-3671
KENTUCKY	Department of Vehicle Regulation, Division of Driver Licensing	State Office Building, 2nd Floor, Frankfort, KY 40622	(502) 564-6800

STATE	AGENCY	ADDRESS	TELEPHONE
LOUISIANA	Department of Public Safety, Office of Motor Vehicles	P.O. Box 64886, Baton Rouge, LA 70896	(504) 925-3720
MAINE	Secretary of State, Motor Vehicle Division	State House, Station 29, August, ME 04333	(207) 287-2386
MARYLAND	Motor Vehicle Administration, Division of Driver Records	6601 Ritchie Highway NE, Glen Burnie, MD 21062	(410) 768-7659
MASSACHUSETTS	Registry of Motor Vehicles, Attn: Suspensions	1135 Tremont Street, Boston, MA 02120	(617) 351-7200
MICHIGAN	Department of State, Bureau of Driver and Vehicle Records	7064 Crowner Drive, Lansing, MI 48918	(517) 322-1571
MINNESOTA	Driver & Vehicle Services Division	Transportation Building, Room 108, 395 John Ireland Blvd., St. Paul, MN 55155	(612) 297-2442
MISSISSIPPI	Department of Public Safety, Bureau of Driver Services,	P.O. Box 958 Jackson, MS 39205	(601) 987-1200
MISSOURI	Drivers License Bureau	P.O. Box 200, Jefferson City, MO 65105	(573) 751-4475
MONTANA	Motor Vehicle Division, Driver Services Bureau, Driver Licensing Records Section	303 N. Roberts Street, Helena, MT 59620	(406) 444-4590
NEBRASKA	Department of Motor Vehicles, Driver Records Section	P.O. Box 94789, Lincoln, NE 68509	(402) 471-3985

STATE	AGENCY	ADDRESS	TELEPHONE
NEVADA	Department of Motor Vehicles, Records Services Section	555 Wright Way, Carson City, NV 89711-0300	(702) 687-5505
NEW HAMPSHIRE	Division of Motor Vehicles, Records Section	James H. Hayes Safety Building, Hazen Drive, Concord, NH 03305	(602) 271-3109
NEW JERSEY	Division of Motor Vehicles, Driver Record Abstract Section	CN-142, 120 S. Stockton Street, Trenton, NJ 08666	(609) 292-6500
NEW MEXICO	Division of Motor Vehicles, Driver Services Bureau	P.O. Box 1028, Santa Fe, NM 87504-1028	(505) 827-0582
NEW YORK	Department of Motor Vehicles, Driver Licensing Division	Swan Street Building, Room 221, Empire State Plaza, Albany, NY 12228	(518) 474-0735
NORTH CAROLINA	Division of Motor Vehicles, Driver License Division	1100 New Bern Avenue, Raleigh, NC 27697	(919) 715-7000
NORTH DAKOTA	State Highway Department, Driver License & Traffic Safety Division	600 E. Boulevard Avenue, Bismarck, ND 58505	(701) 328-2603
OHIO	Bureau of Motor Vehicles, Driver License Division	P.O. Box 16520, Columbus, OH 43266-0020	(614) 752-7500
OKLAHOMA	Department of Public Safety, Driver Improvement Bureau	P.O. Box 11415, Oklahoma City, OK 73136	(405) 425-2098
OREGON	Motor Vehicles Division, Driver Licensing Section	1905 Lana Avenue NE, Salem, OR 97314	(503) 945-5400
PENNSYLVANIA	Bureau of Driver Licensing, Information Sales Unit	P.O. Box 8691, Harrisburg, PA 17105	(800) 523-6429

STATE	AGENCY	ADDRESS	TELEPHONE
RHODE ISLAND	Division of Motor Vehicles, Operator Control Section	345 Harris Avenue, Room 212, Providence, RI 02909	(401) 277-2994
SOUTH CAROLINA	South Carolina Department of Public Safety, Driver Records	P.O. Box 100178, Columbia, SC 29202-3178	(803) 251-2940
SOUTH DAKOTA	Department of Commerce & Regulation, Driver Improvement Program	118 W. Capitol Avenue, Pierre, SD 57501-2036	(605) 773-6883
TENNESSEE	Department of Safety, Driver Control Division	1150 Foster Avenue, Nashville, TN 37210	(615) 741-3954
TEXAS	Chief Department of Public Safety, Driver Improvement and Control	P.O. Box 4087, Austin, TX 78773	(512) 424-2600
UTAH	Motor Vehicle Division, Motor Vehicle Records Department	P.O. Box 30560, Salt Lake City, UT 84130-0560	(801) 965-4430
VERMONT	Department of Motor Vehicles, Driver Improvement	120 State Street, Montpelier, VT 05603	(802) 828-2050
VIRGINIA	Department of Motor Vehicles, Driver Licensing & Information Division	P.O. Box 27412, Richmond,VA 23269	(804) 367-0538
WASHINGTON	Department of Licensing, Division of Driver Services	Highways-Licenses Building, Olympia, WA 98504	(360) 902-3900
WEST VIRGINIA	Department of Motor Vehicles, Driver Improvement Division	1800 Washington Street, East Charleston, WV 25317	(304) 558-0593

STATE	AGENCY	ADDRESS	TELEPHONE
WISCONSIN	Department of Transportation, Compliance and Restoration Section	P.O. Box 7917, Madison, WI 53707	(608) 266-2261
WYOMING	Department of Transportation, Driver Control, Financial Responsibility Section	P.O. Box 1708, Cheyenne, WY 82003	(307) 777-4800

APPENDIX 5:
AVERAGE AUTOMOBILE INSURANCE PREMIUMS—BY STATE

STATE	AVERAGE PREMIUM EXPENDITURE	RANK	COMBINED	LIABILITY	COLLISION	COMPREHENSIVE
Alabama	$577.86	33	$661.60	$313.60	$246.04	$101.97
Alaska	$750.91	16	$904.05	$464.97	$308.83	$130.26
Arizona	$785.05	12	$869.11	$514.67	$208.00	$146.44
Arkansas	$557.70	34	$663.67	$331.12	$221.97	$110.58
California	$790.70	11	$904.56	$512.27	$254.93	$137.36
Colorado	$751.25	15	$854.87	$481.50	$197.64	$175.72
Connecticut	$899.27	5	$976.97	$605.23	$259.73	$112.01
Delaware	$806.05	8	$873.66	$568.57	$220.25	$84.84

STATE	AVERAGE PREMIUM EXPENDITURE	RANK	COMBINED	LIABILITY	COLLISION	COMPREHENSIVE
District of Columbia	$993.07	2	$1,123.18	$576.46	$354.55	$192.18
Florida	$783.23	13	$823.61	$512.23	$204.53	$106.86
Georgia	$627.47	25	$761.34	$332.55	$299.54	$129.25
Hawaii	$958.69	4	$1,092.57	$726.32	$265.01	$101.24
Idaho	$464.56	47	$556.22	$284.36	$173.29	$98.57
Illinois	$637.98	24	$703.73	$363.09	$226.47	$114.17
Indiana	$548.06	38	$637.22	$335.41	$206.64	$95.16
Iowa	$445.39	50	$507.16	$255.55	$154.28	$97.33
Kansas	$495.26	43	$606.29	$271.31	$175.19	$159.79
Kentucky	$581.05	31	$697.99	$381.18	$223.08	$93.73
Louisiana	$802.17	10	$921.32	$543.35	$243.12	$134.86
Maine	$470.18	46	$538.13	$286.04	$177.90	$74.18
Maryland	$759.44	14	$817.89	$478.22	$229.75	$109.92
Massachusetts	$832.83	7	$914.08	$588.22	$212.74	$113.11
Michigan	$697.38	18	$834.64	$348.49	$346.92	$139.24
Minnesota	$653.98	23	$713.33	$437.10	$155.89	$120.34

STATE	AVERAGE PREMIUM EXPENDITURE	RANK	COMBINED	LIABILITY	COLLISION	COMPREHENSIVE
Mississippi	$604.17	27	$706.40	$333.12	$244.45	$128.83
Missouri	$599.35	29	$681.20	$355.99	$210.15	$115.06
Montana	$478.96	44	$605.52	$275.93	$176.17	$153.43
Nebraska	$475.13	45	$572.91	$262.03	$161.53	$149.36
Nevada	$802.50	9	$912.96	$555.60	$236.97	$120.39
New Hampshire	$621.44	26	$681.30	$371.09	$232.38	$77.83
New Jersey	$1,099.07	1	$1,259.42	$726.86	$364.09	$168.47
New Mexico	$659.80	22	$812.03	$420.68	$235.18	$156.17
New York	$959.83	3	$1,113.21	$654.73	$265.40	$193.07
North Carolina	$518.28	41	$594.79	$350.75	$169.36	$74.69
North Dakota	$401.55	51	$505.97	$214.13	$151.33	$140.51
Ohio	$553.27	36	$609.67	$341.11	$189.58	$78.97
Oklahoma	$545.42	39	$670.87	$333.72	$183.79	$153.36
Oregon	$584.76	30	$660.76	$382.37	$186.57	$91.82
Pennsylvania	$687.43	19	$764.15	$443.57	$219.33	$101.25
Rhode Island	$869.50	6	$1,014.05	$615.83	$281.94	$116.28

STATE	AVERAGE PREMIUM EXPENDITURE	RANK	COMBINED	LIABILITY	COLLISION	COMPREHENSIVE
South Carolina	$601.97	28	$698.30	$396.06	$198.43	$103.81
South Dakota	$448.33	49	$570.86	$261.01	$152.74	$157.10
Tennessee	$556.90	35	$637.68	$313.01	$231.89	$92.78
Texas	$726.05	17	$820.38	$504.88	$176.91	$138.59
Utah	$580.72	32	$671.31	$370.31	$199.33	$101.66
Vermont	$514.17	42	$589.72	$292.10	$212.17	$85.45
Virginia	$549.67	37	$608.87	$358.32	$172.48	$78.07
Washington	$665.88	21	$732.72	$455.97	$177.48	$99.27
West Virginia	$671.25	20	$784.49	$433.37	$235.01	$116.12
Wisconsin	$533.49	40	$586.98	$315.65	$166.42	$104.91
Wyoming	$451.62	48	$590.71	$238.90	$181.56	$170.25

Source: National Association of Insurance Commissioners.

APPENDIX 6:
STATES WITH HIGHEST AVERAGE AUTO LIABILITY PREMIUMS

RANK	1989	1995
1	New Jersey**** ($650)	Hawaii* ($737)
2	California ($519)	New Jersey**** ($662)
3	Connecticut* ($473)	Massachusetts* ($640)
4	Hawaii* ($468)	Rhode Island ($619)
5	Dist. of Columbia**($466)	New York* ($607)
6	Pennsylvania*** ($439)	Connecticut***** ($603)
7	Maryland** ($429)	Delaware**($565)
8	Massachusetts* ($427)	District of Columbia** ($548)
9	Florida* ($421)	Louisiana ($547)

* Mandatory No-Fault State

** Mixed or Hybrid No-fault State

***No-fault made optional 1990

****No-fault made optional 1991

*****No-fault repealed 1993, effective 1994.

APPENDIX 7:
DIRECTORY OF MAJOR CASUALTY AND PROPERTY INSURANCE COMPANIES

COMPANY	TELEPHONE	INSURANCE CODE
Aetna Insurance Co. of Connecticut	(860) 277-0111	050
AIU Insurance Co.	(888) 244-2736	267
Allied Mutual Insurance Co.,	(800) 282-9445	N/A
Allstate Insurance Co.	(800) 386-6126	011
Amco Insurance Co.	(800) 282-9445	N/C
American Casualty Co.	(800) 437-8854	015
American Economy Insurance Co.	(317) 262-6262	053
American Employers Insurance Co.	(617) 725-7033	022
American Family Mutual Insurance Co.	(800) 374-1111	N/A
American Home Assurance Co.	(888) 244-2736	027
American International Ins. Co.	(800) 562-2208	N/A
American States Insurance Co.	(317) 262-6262	054
Anthem Casualty Insurance Co.	(800) 537-5568	N/A
Arbella Mutual Insurance Co.	(617) 328-2428	N/A
Arkwright Mutual Insurance Co.	(781) 890-9300	N/A
Atlanta Casualty Co.	(770) 447-8930	N/A
Atlantic Mutual Insurance Co.	(800) 945-7461	045
Atlas Assurance Co. of America	(609) 888-1300	N/A
Auto-Owners Insurance Co.	(517) 323-1365	N/A

COMPANY	TELEPHONE	INSURANCE CODE
Birmingham Fire Insurance of Pennsylvania	(888) 244-2736	N/A
Buckeye Union Insurance Co.	(800) 669-6076	439
California State Auto Assn.	(415) 563-0828	N/A
Camden Fire Insurance Assn.	(888) 421-2111	073
CIGNA Property & Casualty Ins Co.	(215) 761-1000	004
Citizens Insurance Co. of America	(800) 628-0250	648
Commerce & Industry Insurance Co.	(888) 244-2736	087
Commercial Union Insurance Co.	(617) 725-7033	089
Continental Casualty Co.	(800) 669-6076	097
Continental Insurance Co.	(800) 669-6076	098
Coregis Insurance Co.	(312) 849-5000	N/A
Cumis Insurance Society Inc.	(800) 637-2676	448
Dairyland Insurance Co.	(715) 346-9200	N/A
DeSoto Insurance Co.	(888) 823-9754	N/A
Federal Insurance Co.	(212) 483-4399	124
Fidelity & Deposit Co. of Maryland	(800) 854-6011	N/A
Fire Insurance Exchange	(213) 964-8911	N/A
Firemens Insurance Co. of Newark, New Jersey	(800) 669-6076	132
Foremost Insurance Co.	(800) 527-3907	136
GEICO Indemnity Co.	(800) 848-6502	100
General Accident Ins. Co. of America	(888) 421-2111	622
General Casualty of Wisconsin	(608) 825-5715	N/A
General Insurance Co. of America	(206) 545-5841	140
Georgia Farm Bureau Mutual Ins Co.	(912) 474-8411	N/A
Globe Indemnity Co.	(800) 843-7925	147
Government Employees Insurance Co.	(800) 848-6502	148
Grange Mutual Casualty Co.	(614) 445-2625	N/A
Great American Insurance Co.	(800) 724-7722	154

COMPANY	TELEPHONE	INSURANCE CODE
Great West Casualty Co.	(800) 228-8040	N/A
Hanover Insurance Co.	(508) 855-8000	158
Hartford Accident & Indemnity Co.	(860) 547-4780	161
Hartford Casualty Insurance Co.	(860) 547-4780	N/A
Hartford Fire Insurance Co.	(860) 547-4780	162
Horace Mann Insurance Co.	(800) 999-1030	458
Insurance Co. of North America	(215) 761-1000	173
Insurance Co. of the State of Pennsylvania	(888) 244-2736	175
Integon National Insurance Co.	(800) 468-3466	N/A
Interinsurance Exchange Auto Club So.	(714) 850-5111	N/A
John Deere Insurance Co.	(800) 635-3377	480
Lexington Insurance Co.	(888) 244-2736	N/A
Liberty Insurance Corp.	(800) 526-1547	672
Liberty Mutual Fire Insurance Co.	(800) 526-1547	182
Liberty Mutual Insurance Co.	(800) 526-1547	183
Lumbermens Mutual Casualty Co.	(847) 320-2414	190
Medical Liability Mutual Ins Co.	(212) 576-9850	N/A
Mercury Insurance Co. of California	(213) 964-8911	N/A
Metropolitan Property & Casualty Co.	(800) 854-6011	211
Mid-Century Insurance Co.	(213) 964-8911	N/A
Motors Insurance Corp.	(313) 556-4632	677
National Fire Ins. Co. of Hartford	(800) 669-6076	224
National Indemnity Co.	(402) 536-3000	N/A
National Union Fire Ins. Of Pittsburgh	(888) 244-2736	N/A
Nationwide Mutual Fire Insurance Co.	(800) 421-3535	230
Nationwide Mutual Insurance Co.	(800) 421-3535	231
New Hampshire Insurance Co.	(888) 244-2736	235

COMPANY	TELEPHONE	INSURANCE CODE
New Jersey Manufacturers Ins. Co.	(609) 883-1300	426
North Carolina Farm Bureau Mutual Ins.	(919) 782-1705	N/A
North River Insurance Co.	(800) 690-5520	250
Northern Assurance Co. of America	(617) 725-7033	N/A
Ohio Casualty Insurance Co.	(513) 867-3000	465
Pacific Employers Insurance Co.	(215) 761-1000	423
Pacific Indemnity Co.	(212) 483-4399	268
Phoenix Insurance Co.	(800) 252-4633	282
Preferred Risk Mutual Insurance Co.	(515) 267-5299	288
Progressive Casualty Insurance Co.	(800) 274-4499	413
Progressive Northern Insurance Co.	(800) 274-4499	413
Progressive Northwestern Ins. Co.	(800) 274-4499	413
Progressive Specialty Insurance Co.	(800) 274-4499	413
Protection Mutual Insurance Co.	(847) 825-4474	N/A
Reliance Insurance Co.	(215) 761-1000	N/A
Republic Underwriters Insurance Co.	(214) 559-1270	N/A
Royal Insurance Co. of America	(800) 843-7925	293
Safeco Insurance Co. of America	(206) 545-5841	304
Scottsdale Insurance Co.	(602) 948-0505	N/A
Selective Insurance Co. of America	(973) 948-2900	315
Sentry Insurance	(715) 346-9200	N/A
Shelter Mutual Insurance Co.	(800) 743-5837	N/A
Standard Fire Insurance Co.	(800) 252-4633	325
State Farm Fire & Casualty Co.	(800) 732-5246	327
State Farm Indemnity Co.	(800) 732-5246	N/A
State Farm Lloyds	(800) 732-5246	N/A
State Farm Mutual Automobile Ins. Co.	(800) 732-5246	328
Travelers Indemnity Co.	(860) 277-0111	344

COMPANY	TELEPHONE	INSURANCE CODE
Trinity Universal Insurance Co.	(214) 360-8039	N/A
United Services Automobile Assn.	(800) 531-8222	355
United States Fire Insurance Co.	(800) 690-5520	358
USAA Casualty Insurance Co.	(800) 531-8222	356
Utica Mutual Insurance Co.	(800) 695-1914	364
Vesta Fire Insurance Corp.	(800) 444-3928	N/A
Vigilant Insurance Co.	(212) 483-4399	368
Westfield Insurance Co.	(800) 443-3311	N/A
Zenith Insurance Co.	(800) 440-5020	N/A

Source: New York Lawyers Diary and Manual.

APPENDIX 8:
STATES WITH HIGHEST GROWTH IN
AVERAGE AUTO LIABILITY PREMIUMS
(1989-1995)

RANK	1989-1995	GROWTH
1	South Dakota**	78.6%
2	Nebraska	68.2%
3	Texas**	67.4%
4	Kentucky**	65.8%
5	West Virginia	62.9%
6	Utah*	61.4%
7	Hawaii*	57.5%
8	New York*	56.8%
9	New Mexico	53.3%
10	Rhode Island	51.8%
11	Wyoming	50.9%
12	Massachusetts*	49.9%
13	Delaware**	49.1%
14	Oklahoma	49.0%
15	Colorado*	49.0%

* Mandatory No-fault State

** Hybrid No-fault State

APPENDIX 9:
NUMBER OF NO-FAULT STATES AMONG TOP 10 STATES WITH MOST EXPENSIVE AUTOMOBILE INSURANCE RATES (1987-1995)

YEAR	RANK
1987	9
1988	8
1989	8
1990	8
1991	8
1992	7
1993	7
1994	6
1995	6

APPENDIX 10:
NEW YORK STATE VERBAL THRESHOLD FOR RECOVERY OF NON-ECONOMIC DAMAGES

SECTION 5102. DEFINITIONS

§5102(d). "Serious injury" means a personal injury which results in death; dismemberment; significant disfigurement; a fracture; loss of a fetus; permanent loss of use of a body organ, member, function or system; permanent consequential limitation of use of a body organ or member; significant limitation of use of a body function or system; or a medically determined injury or impairment of a non-permanent nature which prevents the injured person from performing substantially all of the material acts which constitute such person's usual and customary daily activities for not less than ninety days during the one hundred eighty days immediately following the occurrence of the injury or impairment.

Source: § 5102(d) of McKinney's Consolidated Laws of New York Annotated, Insurance Law, Book 27, West Publishing Company, 1993.

APPENDIX 11:
NO-FAULT RESTRICTIONS ON PAIN AND SUFFERING LAWSUITS

TORT	CO	FL	HI	KS	KY	MA	MI	MN	NJ	NY	ND	PA	UT
Death	Yes	Yes	Yes	Yes	Yes	Yes	Yes	Yes	Yes	Yes	Yes	n/a	Yes
Dismemberment	Yes	n/a	Yes	Yes	Yes	n/a	n/a	Yes	Yes	Yes	Yes	Yes	Yes
Loss of bodily function	n/a	Yes	Yes	Yes	n/a	Yes	Yes	n/a	Yes	Yes	n/a	n/a	n/a
Serious disfigurement	Yes	Yes	Yes	Yes	Yes	Yes	Yes	Yes	Yes	Yes	Yes	n/a	Yes
Permanent injury or disability	Yes	Yes	n/a	Yes	Yes	Yes	Yes	Yes	Yes	Yes	Yes	n/a	Yes

TORT	CO	FL	HI	KS	KY	MA	MI	MN	NJ	NY	ND	PA	UT
Fracture	n/a	n/a	n/a	n/a	n/a	Yes	n/a	n/a	n/a	Yes	n/a	n/a	n/a
Serious fracture	n/a	n/a	n/a	Yes	Yes	Yes	n/a	n/a	Yes	Yes	n/a	n/a	n/a
Temporary disability or loss of earning capacity	Yes	n/a	Yes	n/a	n/a	n/a	n/a	Yes	n/a	Yes	Yes	n/a	n/a
Dollar threshold	$2,500	Verbal	$5,000	$2,000	$1,000	$2,000	Verbal	$4,000	Choice or verbal	Verbal	Choice	Choice	$3,000

Source: American Insurance Association.

APPENDIX 12:
SUBROGATION AGREEMENT IN CONNECTION WITH A CLAIM UNDER MOTOR VEHICLE NO-FAULT INSURANCE LAW

DATE:

TO: [Name and Address of Applicant]

RE: [Name of Policyholder and Policy Number; Date of Accident; Insurance Company File Number]

FROM: [Name of Insurer's Claim Representative; Insurance Company; Address; Phone Number]

Dear Applicant:

Kindly complete and return this agreement at once. Failure to do so may delay payment of your No-Fault benefits.

SUBROGATION AGREEMENT

To: [Name of Insurer] (hereinafter "Company")

The undersigned hereby declares that a bodily injury was sustained by [name of applicant] on [date of accident] and a claim for extended economic loss benefits, including medical, loss of earnings, and other reasonable and necessary expenses and/or a death benefit, is being made under Policy Number [number] issued to [name of insured].

In consideration for benefits paid or payable under the additional personal injury protection endorsement of the foregoing policy, it is agreed that:

1. In accordance with the provisions of the policy, the Company is subrogated to the extent of any payment for additional first-party benefits to the rights of the applicant against any person who may be liable

to the injured person because of bodily injury with respect to which additional personal injury protection benefits are afforded under this policy.

2. The undersigned shall cooperate with the Company and upon the Company's request, assist in the conduct of suits and in enforcing any Company right of subrogation for additional personal injury protection benefits paid against any person who may be liable to the injured person because of bodily injury with respect to which additional personal injury protection benefits are afforded under this policy.

3. The undersigned to or for whom payments are made or the undersigned's legal representative will notify the Company in writing prior to institution of any legal proceedings against any person legally responsible for the above described bodily injury and will do whatever is necessary to secure and to do nothing to prejudice the Company's subrogation rights.

I have carefully read the foregoing subrogation agreement, understand its contents , and have signed the same as my free act.

Date:_____

BY: [Signature of Applicant]

APPENDIX 13:
EXCERPTS FROM THE MICHIGAN
NO-FAULT INSURANCE STATUTES

MICHIGAN COMPILED LAWS

CHAPTER 500—MOTOR VEHICLE PERSONAL AND PROPERTY PROTECTION

§ 500.3101. Security Required for Motor Vehicles; Definitions

§ 3101(1). The owner or registrant of a motor vehicle required to be registered shall maintain security for personal protection insurance, property protection insurance, and residual liability insurance. Security shall only be required to be in effect during the period the motor vehicle is driven or moved upon a highway. Notwithstanding any other provision in this act, an insurer that has issued an automobile insurance policy on a motor vehicle that is not driven or moved upon a highway may allow the insured owner or registrant of the motor vehicle to delete a portion of the coverage under the policy and maintain the comprehensive coverage portion of the policy in effect.

§ 3101(2). [This section contains definitions].

§ 3101(3). Security may be provided under a policy issued by an insurer duly authorized to transact business which affords insurance for the payment of benefits described in subsection (1). A policy of insurance represented or sold as providing security shall be deemed to provide insurance for the payment of the benefits.

§ 3101(4). Security required by subsection (1) may be provided by any other method approved by the secretary of state as affording security equivalent to that afforded by a policy of insurance, if proof of the security is filed and continuously maintained with the secretary of state through the period the motor vehicle is driven or moved upon a highway. The person filing the security has all the obligations and rights of an insurer under this chapter. When the context permits, "insurer" as used in this chapter, includes any person filing the security as provided in this section.

§ 500.3101a. Certificates of Insurance

§ 3101a(1). An insurer, in conjunction with the issuance of an automobile insurance policy, as defined in section 3303, shall provide 2 certificates of insurance to each policyholder. The insurer shall mark 1 of the certificates as the secretary of state's copy, which copy shall be filed with the secretary of state by the policyholder upon application for a vehicle registration. The secretary of state shall not maintain the certificate of insurance received under this subsection on file.

§ 3101a(1). [This section pertains to criminal penalties for supplying false information or issuing or using an invalid certificate.]

§ 500.3102. Nonresident Vehicle; Penalties; Annual Statistical Report

§ 3102(1). [A nonresident owner or registrant of a motor vehicle or motorcycle must maintain security for the payment of benefits if vehicle is in Michigan more than 30 days in any year.]

§ 3102(2). [This section pertains to criminal penalties for operating a motor vehicle or motorcycle without having required security in effect.]

§ 3102(3). [Rebuttable presumption for criminal proceeding.]

§ 500.3103. Security Required for Motorcycles; Statistical Report

§ 3103(1). An owner or registrant of a motorcycle shall provide security against loss resulting from liability imposed by law for property damage, bodily injury, or death suffered by a person arising out of the ownership, maintenance, or use of that motorcycle. The security shall conform with the requirements of section 3009(1).

§ 3103(2). [Each insurer transacting business in Michigan which offers liability coverage under (1) shall offer security for the payment of first party medical payments in increments of $5,000. Such an insurer may offer deductibles and other provisions applicable to benefits to persons who are named insureds, spouses of named insureds, and relatives of named insureds domiciled in the same household, if approved by the commissioner of insurance.]

§ 500.3104. Catastrophic Claims Association

§ 3104. [This section provides for the establishment of the "catastrophic claims association", an unincorporated nonprofit association. Each insurer writing insurance coverage which provide the security required in Michigan shall be a member of the association and shall be indemnified for all of the loss not including claim expenses which it sustains in excess of $250,000. The section, which is very lengthy (6 pages) sets forth the powers and duties of the association and its members.

§ 500.3105. Accidental Bodily Injury

§ 3105(1). Under personal protection insurance an insurer is liable to pay benefits for accidental bodily injury arising out of the ownership, operation, maintenance or use of a motor vehicle, subject to the provisions of this chapter.

§ 3105(2). Personal protection insurance benefits are due under this chapter without regard to fault.

§ 3105(3). Bodily injury includes death resulting therefrom and damage to or loss of a person's prosthetic devices in connection with the injury.

§ 3105(4). Bodily injury is accidental as to a person claiming personal protection benefits unless suffered intentionally by the injured person or caused intentionally by the claimant. Even though a person knows that bodily injury is substantially certain to be caused by his act or omission, he does not cause or suffer injury intentionally if he acts or refrains from acting for the purpose of averting injury to property or to any person including himself.

§ 500.3106. Parked Vehicles

§ 3106(1). Accidental bodily injury does not arise out of the ownership, operation, maintenance, or use of a parked vehicle as a motor carrier unless any of the following occur:

(a) The vehicle was parked in such a way as to cause unreasonable risk of the bodily injury which occurred;

(b) Except as provided in subsection (2), the injury was a direct result of physical contact with equipment permanently mounted on the vehicle, while the equipment was being operated or used, or property being lifted onto or lowered from the vehicle in the loading or unloading process.

(C) Except as provided in subsection (2), the injury was sustained by a person while occupying, entering into, or alighting from the vehicle.

§ 3106(2). Accidental bodily injury does not arise out of the ownership, operation, maintenance, or use of a parked vehicle as a motor vehicle if benefits [are available to an employee under a workers compensation law].

§ 500.3107. Personal Protection Insurance Benefits

§ 3107(a). Allowable expenses consisting of all reasonable charges incurred for reasonable necessary products, services and accommodations for an injured person's care, recovery, or rehabilitation. Allowable expenses within personal protection insurance coverage shall not include charges for hospital room in excess of a reasonable and customary charge for semiprivate accommodations except when the injured person requires special or intensive care ... Beginning October 1, 1988, benefits for funeral and burial expenses shall be payable in the amount set forth in the policy but shall not be less than $1,750.00 nor more than $5,000.00.

§ 3107(b). Work loss consisting of loss of income from work an injured person would have performed during the first 3 years after the date of the accident if he or she had not been injured and expenses not exceeding $20.00 per day, reasonably incurred in obtaining ordinary and necessary services in lieu of those that, if he or she had not been injured, an injured person would have performed during the first 3 years after the date of the accident, not for income but for the benefit of himself or herself or his or her dependent. Work loss does not include any loss after the date on which the injured person dies. [Benefits for loss of income shall be reduced 15 percent because such benefits are not taxable income, unless claimant presents to the insurer reasonable proof of a lower value of the income tax advantage.] Beginning March 30, 1973, the benefits payable for work loss sustained in a single 30-day period and the income earned by an injured person for work during the same period together shall not exceed $1,000.00, which maximum shall apply to any lesser period of work loss. Beginning October 1, 1974, the maximum shall be adjusted annually to reflect changes in the cost of living under rules prescribed by the commissioner but any change in the maximum shall apply only to benefits arising out of accidents occurring subsequent to the date of change in the maximum.

§ 500.3107a. Work Loss Basis

§ 3107a. Subject to the provisions of section 3107(b), work loss for an injured person who is temporarily unemployed at the time of the accident or during the period of disability shall be based on earned income for the last month employed full time preceding the accident.

---

§ 500.3108 Survivor's Benefits

§ 3108(1). Except as provided in subsection (2), personal protection insurance benefits are payable for a survivor's loss which consists of a loss, after the date on which the deceased died, of contributions of tangible things of economic value, not including services, that dependents of the deceased at the time of the deceased's death would have received for support during their dependency from the deceased if the deceased had not suffered the accidental bodily injury causing death and expenses, not exceeding $20.00 per day, reasonably incurred by these dependents during their dependency and after the date on which the deceased died in obtaining ordinary and necessary services in lieu of those that the deceased would have performed for their benefit if the deceased had not suffered the injury causing death. Except as provided in section (2) the benefits payable for a survivor's loss in connection with the death of a person in a single 30-day period . . . shall not exceed $1,475.00 for accidents occurring on of after October 1, 1978, and is not payable beyond the first three years after the date of the accident.

§ 3108(2). The maximum payable shall be adjusted annually to reflect changes in the cost of living under rules prescribed by the commissioner. A change in the maximum shall apply only to benefits arising out of accidents occurring subsequent to the date of change in the maximum. The maximum shall apply to the aggregate benefits for all survivors payable under this section on account of the death of any one person.

§ 500.3109 State or Federal Benefits

§ 3109(1). Benefits provided or required to be provided under the laws of any state or the federal government shall be subtracted from the personal protection insurance benefits otherwise payable for the injury.

§ 3109(2). An injured person is a natural person suffering accidental bodily injury.

§ 3109(3). An insurer providing personal protection insurance benefits may offer, at appropriately reduced premium rates, a deductible of a specified dollar amount which does not exceed $300 per accident. This deductible may be applicable to all or any specified types of personal protection insurance benefits but shall apply only to benefits payable to the person named in the policy, his spouse and any relative of either domiciled in the same household. Any other deductible provisions require the prior approval of the commissioner.

§ 500.3109a. Deductibles and Exclusions

§ 3109a. An insurer providing personal protection insurance benefits shall offer, at appropriately reduced premium rates, deductibles and exclusions reasonably related to other health and accident coverage on the insured. The deductibles and exclusions required to be offered by this section shall be subject to prior approval by the commissioner and shall apply only to benefits payable to the person named in the policy, the spouse of the insured and any relative or either domiciled in the same household.

§ 500.3110. Dependents; Accrual of Benefits

§ 3110(1). This subsection defines the persons who are conclusively presumed to be dependents of a deceased person.]

§ 3110(2). In all other cases, questions of dependency and the extent of dependency shall be determined in accordance with the facts as they exist at the time of death.

§ 3110(3). [This subsection defines when dependency terminates for a surviving spouse or any other person.]

§ 3110(4). Personal protection insurance benefits payable for accidental bodily injury accrue not when the injury occurs but as the allowable expense, work loss or survivors' loss is incurred.

§ 500.3111. Accidents Occurring Out of State

§ 3111. Personal protection insurance benefits are payable for accidental bodily injury suffered in an accident occurring out of this state, if the accident occurs within the United States, its territories and possessions or in Canada, and the person whose injury is the basis of the claim was at the time of the accident a named insured under a personal protection insurance policy, his spouse, a relative of either domiciled in the same household or an occupant of a vehicle involved in the accident whose owner or registrant was insured under a personal protection insurance policy or has provided security approved by the secretary of state under subsection (4) of section 3101.

§ 500.3112. Payment of Personal Protection Insurance Benefits

§ 3112. Personal protection insurance benefits are payable to or for the benefit of an injured person or, in the case of his death, to or for the benefit of his dependents. Payment by an insurer in good faith of personal protection insurance benefits, to or for the benefit of a person who it believe is entitled to the benefits, discharges the insurer's liability to the extent of the payments unless the insurer has been notified in writing on the claim of some other person. [In case of doubt, an insurer or any other interested person may apply to the circuit court for an appropriate order. The court is authorized to designate the payee and make an equitable apportionment. Unless a court orders otherwise, the insurer is authorized to pay the dependents of a decedent the personal protection insurance benefits that accrued to him before his death and to pay the surviving spouse the benefits due any dependent children.]

§ 500.3113. Exemptions From Payment

§ 3113. A person is not entitled to be paid personal protection insurance benefits for accidental bodily injury if at the time of the accident any of the following circumstances existed:

(a) [Victim was using a stolen motor vehicle or motorcycle.]

(b) [Victim was the owner or registrant of an uninsured motor vehicle which was involved in the accident.]

(c) [Out-of-state victim occupying an out-of-state vehicle which was not insured by an insurer that has filed a "certification in compliance" in Michigan under section 3163.]

§ 500.3114. Beneficiaries

§ 3114. [Subsection (1) sets forth the general rule that a no-fault policy "applies to accidental bodily injury to the person named in the policy, the person's spouse, and a relative of either domiciled in the same household, if the injury arises from a motor vehicle accident."]

[Subsection (2) provides that an injured person who occupied a motor vehicle in the business of transporting passengers is entitled to receive no-fault benefits from the insurer of that vehicle, unless he or she was a passenger on a school bus, a common-carrier bus, or an insured taxicab, unless he or she was not entitled to no-fault benefits under any other policy in which case the commercial vehicle is still responsible.]

[Subsection (3) provides that an employee, his or her spouse, or a relative of either domiciled in the same household who were injured while occupying a vehicle owned by or registered to his or her employer is entitled to no-fault benefits from the insurer of the furnished vehicle.]

[Subsections (4) and (5) set forth the orders of priority of payment when more than one insurer is obligated to pay no-fault benefits.]

[Subsection (6) grants an insurer which pays benefits a right of partial recoupment against other insurers in the same order of priority.]

§ 500.3115. Priority of Claims: Accidental Bodily Injury

§ 3115. [This section sets forth the rules for recovery of no-fault benefits by pedestrians who are not no-fault insureds themselves (in which case they would recover benefits from their own no-fault insurers).]

[Subsection (1) provides that an injured pedestrian ("a person suffering accidental bodily injury while not an occupant of a motor vehicle") shall receive no-fault benefits from, first, insurers of owners or registrants of vehicles involved in the accident, and, second, from insurers of operators of vehicles involved in the accident.]

[Under subsection (2), an insurer which pays benefits is entitled to receive partial recoupment from other insurers in the same order of priority, plus a reasonable amount for its processing costs.]

[Subsection (3) provides that a limit upon the amount of no-fault benefits shall be determined without regard to the number of policies applicable to the accident.]

§ 500.3116. Indemnification of Personal Protection Insurers

§ 3116(1). A subtraction from personal protection insurance benefits shall not be made because of the value of a claim in tort based on the same accidental bodily injury.

[Subsection (2) authorizes an insurer who paid no-fault benefits to a claimant to recover some or all of that amount if the claimant later recovers damages in a tort claim. The amount of the subtraction or reimbursement can only be for damages for which the claimant has received or is eligible to receive no-fault benefits "exclusive of reasonable attorneys' fees and other reasonable expenses incurred in effecting the recovery."]

[Subsection (3) provides that an insurer who is entitled to reimbursement but did not receive it from a claimant in a tort claim is entitled to indemnity from the person who, with notice of the insurer's interest, made the payment to that claimant.]

§ 3116(4). A subtraction or reimbursement shall not be due the claimant's insurer from that portion of any recovery to the extent that recovery is realized for noneconomic loss as provided in section 3135(1) and (2)(b) or for allowable expenses, work loss, and survivor's loss as defined in Section 3107 to 3110 in excess of the amount recovered by the claimant by his or her insurer.

§ 500.3121. Property Protection Benefits

§ 3121. [This section creates a form of no-fault property damage insurance known as "property protection insurance".]

§ 500.3123. Exclusions

§ 3123. [This section excludes damages to specified kinds of property from property protection insurance benefits.]

§ 500.3125. Priority of Claims: Accidental Property Damage

§ 3125. [This section sets the same priority for payment of no-fault property claims as other sections provide for no-fault personal injury claims: first priority—insurers of owners or registrants of involved vehicles; second priority—insurers of operators of involved vehicles.]

§ 500.3127. Indemnification of Property Insurers

§ 3123. [The recoupment and indemnification provisions of the Act as to no-fault personal injury insurers are incorporated by reference as to no-fault property protection insurers.]

§ 500.3131. Residual Liability Coverage

§ 3131(1). Residual liability insurance shall cover bodily injury and property damage which occurs within the United States, its territories and possessions, or in Canada. This insurance shall afford coverage equivalent to that required as evidence of automobile liability insurance under the financial responsibility laws of the place in which the injury or damage occurs. In this state this insurance shall afford coverage for automobile liability retained by section 3135.

§ 3131(2). This section shall not require coverage in this state other than that required by section 3009(1) . . . [Michigan requires each motorist to maintain $20,000/$40,000/$10,000 in liability coverage.]

§ 500.3135. Tort Liability

§ 3135(1). A person remains subject to tort liability for noneconomic loss caused by his ownership, maintenance or use of a motor vehicle only if the injured person has suffered death, serious impairment of body function or permanent serious disfigurement.

§ 3135(2). Notwithstanding any other provision of law, tort liability arising from the ownership, maintenance or use within this state of a motor vehicle with respect to which the security required by section 3101(3) and (4) was in effect is abolished except as to:

(a) Intentionally caused harm to persons or property. . .

(b) Damages for noneconomic loss as provided and limited in subsection (1).

(c) Damages for allowable expenses, work loss and survivor's loss as defined in sections 3107 to 3110 in excess of the daily, monthly and 3-year limitations contained in those sections. The party liable for damages is entitled to an exemption reducing his or her liability by the amount of taxes that would have been payable on account of income the injured person would have received if he or she had not been injured.

(d) Damages up to $400.00 to motor vehicles, to the extent that the damages are not covered by insurance . . .

§ 3135(3). [This subsection sets forth the rules which shall govern a tort action, under subsection (2)(d), for property damage.]

§ 3135(4). [This subsection identifies the courts where tort actions under subsection (2)(d) for property damage shall be commenced and authorizes a judge to assess costs if such an action is removed to a higher court.]

§ 3135(5). [This subsection provides that a decision made pursuant to subsection (2)(d) shall not be res judicata as to any other liability determination.]

§ 3135(6). [Effective date of property tort action subsections.]

§ 500.3141. Notice of Accident

§ 3141. An insurer may require a written notice to be given as soon as practicable after an accident involving a motor vehicle with respect to which the policy affords the security required by this chapter.

§ 500.3142. Overdue Personal Protection Benefits

§ 3142(1). Personal protection insurance benefits are payable as loss accrues.

§ 3142(2). Personal protection insurance benefits are overdue if not paid within 30 days after an insurer received reasonable proof of the fact and of the amount of loss sustained. If reasonable proof is not supplied as to the entire claim, the amount supported by reasonable proof is overdue if not paid within 30 days after the proof is received by the insurer. For the purpose of calculating the extent to which benefits are overdue, payment shall be treated as made on the date a draft or other valid instrument was placed in the United States mail in a properly addressed, postpaid envelope, or, if not so posted, on the date of delivery.

§ 3142(3). An overdue payment bears simple interest at the rate of 12 percent per annum.

§ 500.3143. Assignment of Future Benefits

§ 3143. An agreement for assignment of a right to benefits payable in the future is void.

§ 500.3145. Limitation of Actions: Recovery of Benefits

§ 3145(1). An action for recovery of personal protection insurance benefits payable under this chapter for accidental bodily injury may not be commenced later than 1 year after the date of the accident causing the injury unless written notice of injury as provided herein has been given to the insurer within 1 year after the accident or unless the insurer has previously made a payment of personal protection insurance benefits for the injury. . . . The notice shall give the name and address of the claimant and indicate in ordinary language the name of the person injured and the time, place and nature of his injury.

§ 3145(2). [Statute of limitation for property no-fault benefits.]

§ 500.3146. Limitation of Actions: Indemnity

§ 3146. An action by an insurer to enforce its rights of recovery or indemnity under section 500.3116 may not be commenced later than 1 year after payment has been received by a claimant upon a tort claim with respect to which the insurer has a right of reimbursement or recovery under section 3116.

§ 500.3148. Attorneys' Fees

§ 3148(1). An attorney is entitled to a reasonable fee for advising and representing a claimant in an action for personal or property protection insurance benefits which are overdue . . .

§ 3148(2). An insurer may be allowed by a court an award of a reasonable sum against a claimant that was in some respect fraudulent or so excessive as to have no reasonable foundation . . .

§500.3151. Medical Examinations

§ 3151. When the mental or physical condition of a person is material to a claim that has been or may be made for past or future personal protection insurance benefits, the person shall submit to a mental or physical examination by physicians. A personal protection insurer may include reasonable provisions in a personal protection insurance policy for mental and physical examination of persons claiming personal protection insurance benefits.

§ 500.3152. Reports of Medical Examination

§ 3152. If requested by a person examined, a party causing an examination to be made shall deliver to him a copy of every written report concerning the examination rendered by an examining physician, at least 1 of which reports shall set out his findings and conclusions in detail. After such request and delivery, the party causing the examination to be made is entitled upon request to receive from the person examined every written report available to him or his representative concerning any examination relevant to the claim, previously or thereafter made, of the same mental or physical condition, and the names and addresses of physicians and medical care facilities rendering diagnoses or treatment in regard to the injury or to a relevant past injury, and shall authorize the insurer to inspect and copy records of physicians, hospitals, clinics or other medical facilities relevant to the claim. By requesting and obtaining a report of the examination so ordered or by taking the deposition of the examiner, the person examined waives any privilege he may have, in relation to the claim for benefits, regarding the testimony of every other person who has examined or may thereafter examine him in respect of the same mental or physical condition.

§500.3153. Refusal to Submit to Medical Examination

§ 3153. A court may make such orders in regard to the refusal to comply with sections 3151 and 3152 as are just, except that an order shall not be entered directing the arrest of a person for disobeying an order to submit to a physical or mental examination. The orders that may be made in regard to such a refusal include, but are not limited to:

(a) An order that the mental or physical conditions of the disobedient party shall be taken to be established for the purposes of the claim in accordance with the contention of the party obtaining the order.

(b) An order refusing to allow the disobedient person to support or oppose designated claims or defenses, or prohibiting him from introducing evidence of mental or physical condition.

(c) An order rendering judgment by default against the disobedient person as to his entire claim or a designated part of it.

(d) An order requiring the disobedient person to reimburse the insurer for reasonable attorney's fees and expenses incurred in defense against the claim.

(e) An order requiring delivery of a report [of a medical examination] on such terms as are just, and if a physician fails or refuses to make the report a court may exclude his testimony if offered at trial.

§ 500.3157. Medical Services Charges

§ 3157. A physician, hospital, clinic or other person or institution lawfully rendering treatment to an injured person for an accidental bodily injury covered by personal protection insurance, and a person or institution providing rehabilitative occupational training following the injury, may charge a reasonable amount for the products, services and accommodations rendered. The charge shall not exceed the amount the person or institution customarily charges for like products, services and accommodations in cases not involving insurance.

§ 500.3158. Record of Medical Treatment; Earnings Statement

§ 3158(1). [An employer shall furnish a sworn statement of the pre- and post-accident earnings of an injured person, when requested to do so by a no-fault insurer against whom a claim has been made based upon that person's injury.]

§ 3158(2). [Upon request by a no-fault insurer against whom a claim has been made, a physician or medical institution which has provided any product, service or accommodation related to any injury or any condition claimed to be connected to any injury as to which that no-fault claim has been made] (a) shall furnish forthwith a written report of the history, condition, treatment and dates and costs of treatment of the injured person and (b) shall produce forthwith and permit inspection and copying of its record regarding the history, condition, treatment and dates and costs of treatment.

§ 500.3159. Order for Discovery

§ 3159. [A court may enter an order of discovery, on motion for good cause shown upon notice to all interested persons, when there is a dispute regarding an insurer's right to discover facts about an injured person's earnings or about his history, condition, treatment, and dates and costs of treatment. If such an order is granted, the court shall specify the time, place, manner, condition, and scope of the discovery. The court may refuse discovery, specify conditions of discovery, and order payment of costs and expenses including reasonable attorneys fees.]

§500.3163. Certification

§ 3163(1). An insurer authorized to transact liability insurance and personal and property protection insurance in this state shall file and maintain a written certification that any accidental bodily injury or property damage occurring in this state arising from the ownership, operation, maintenance or use of a motor vehicle as a motor vehicle by an out-of-state resident who is insured under its automobile liability insurance policies, shall be subject to the personal and property protection insurance system set forth in this act.

§ 3163(2). A nonadmitted insurer may voluntarily file the certification described in subsection (1).

§ 3163(3). [When a filed certification applies to accidental bodily injury or property damage, the insurer and its insureds have the rights and immunities of no-fault insureds and claimants have the rights and benefits of no-fault claimants.]

§ 500.3171. Assigned Claims Facility

§ 3171. The secretary of state shall organize and maintain an assigned claims facility and plan. A self-insurer and insurer writing insurance as provided in this chapter in this state shall participate in the assigned claims plan. Costs incurred in the operation of the facility and the plan shall be allocated fairly among insurers and self-insurers. The secretary of state shall promulgate rules to implement the facility and plan in accordance with and subject to [specified laws].

§500.3172. Beneficiaries of Assigned Claims Plan

§ 3172. This section describes the situations in which persons entitled to claim no-fault benefits may receive such benefits through an assigned claims plan. The section specifies that the amount of the benefits payable through such a plan shall be reduced to the extent that benefits covering the same loss are available from other sources. If there is a dispute between two or more no-fault insurers concerning their obligation to provide benefits or the equitable distribution of loss, the claim shall be assigned to the assigned claims facility which shall assign it to an insurer and that insurer shall immediately commence an action in circuit court joining as parties each insurer to the disputed obligation or distribution. The circuit court shall determine the rights and duties of any interested party and shall order reimbursement from the applicable insurer or insurers to the extent of their responsibility, as determined by the court. Reimbursement shall be of all benefits and costs paid or incurred by the assigned claims facility and all benefits and costs paid or incurred by insurers determined not to be obligated to provide no-fault benefits, including reasonable attorney fees and interest.]

§ 500.3173. Disqualified Persons

§ 3173. A person who . . . is disqualified from receiving personal protection insurance benefits under a policy otherwise applying to his accidental bodily injury is also disqualified from receiving benefits under the assigned claims plan.

§ 500.3173a. Determination of Eligibility

§ 3173a. The assigned claims facility shall make an initial determination of the claimant's eligibility for benefits under the assigned claims plan and shall deny an obviously ineligible claim. The claimant shall be notified promptly in writing of the denial and the reasons for the denial.

§ 500.3174. Notice of Claim

§ 3174. A person claiming through an assigned claim plan shall notify the [assigned claim] facility of his claim within the time that would have been allowed for filing an action for personal protection benefits if identifiable coverage applicable to the claim had been in effect. The facility shall promptly assigned the claim in accordance with the plan and notify the claimant of the identity and address of the insurer to which the claim is assigned, of the facility if the claim is assigned to it. An action by the claimant shall not be commenced more than 30 days after receipt of notice of the assignment or the last date on which the action could have been commenced against an insurer of identifiable coverage applicable to the claim, whichever is later.

§ 500.3175. Assignment of Claims

§ 3175(1). The assignment of claim shall be made according to rules that assure fair allocation of the burden of assigned claims among insurers doing business in this state on a basis reasonably related to the volume of automobile liability and personal protection insurance they write on motor vehicles or of the number of self-insured motor vehicles. An insurer to whom claims have been assigned shall make prompt payment of loss in accordance with this act and is thereupon entitled to reimbursement by the assigned claims facility for the payments and the established loss adjustment cost, together with [a formula amount based on the average annual 90-day U.S. treasury bill yield rate].

§ 3175(2). The insurer to whom claims have been assigned shall preserve and enforce rights to indemnity or reimbursement against third parties and account to the assigned claims facility therefor and shall assign such rights to the assigned claims facility upon reimbursement by the assigned claims facility. This section shall not preclude an insurer from entering into reasonable compromises and settlements with third parties against whom rights to indemnity or reimbursement exist . . .

§ 3175(3). [Statute of limitations for actions to enforce rights to indemnity or reimbursement against a third party.]

§ 3175(4). Payments for the operation of the assigned claims facility and plan not paid by the due date shall bear interest at the rate of 20 percent per annum.

§ 3175(5). [Debtor can pay his debt to the facility in installments.]

§ 500.3176. Costs

§ 3176. Reasonable costs incurred in the handling and disposition of assigned claims . . . shall be taken into account in making and regulating rates for automobile liability and personal protection insurance.

§ 500.3177. Subrogation

§ 3177(1). [An insurer obligated to pay no-fault benefits for an injury may recover the benefits paid and appropriate loss adjustment costs from the owner or registrant of the uninsured motor vehicle. If such owner or registrant fails to pay that amount within 30 days, his or her motor vehicle registration and license may be suspended or revoked. For purposes of this section, an uninsured motor vehicle means one as to which applicable no-fault insurance as required by sections 3101 and 3102 is not in effect at the time of the accident.]

§ 3177(2). The motor vehicle registration and license shall not be suspended or revoked . . . if the debtor enters into a written agreement with the secretary of state permitting the payment of the judgment in installments. . .

§ 3177(3). The secretary of state . . . shall notify the owner or registrant of an uninsured vehicle of the provisions of subsection (1) . . . and inform that person of the right to enter into a written agreement . . . for the payment of the judgment or debt in installments.

§ 500.3179. Applicability of Provisions

§ 3179. [This section provides that the original Michigan no-fault law applied to accidents that occurred on or after October 1, 1973.]

APPENDIX 14:
NEW YORK MOTOR VEHICLE NO-FAULT INSURANCE LAW ARBITRATION REQUEST FORM

NEW YORK MOTOR VEHICLE NO-FAULT INSURANCE LAW
ARBITRATION REQUEST FORM

(FOR PERSONAL INJURIES SUSTAINED ON AND AFTER 12/1/77)

OPTIONAL NO-FAULT ARBITRATION IS FINAL AND BINDING EXCEPT FOR THE LIMITED GROUNDS FOR REVIEW SET FORTH IN THE LAW AND REGULATIONS. UPON RECEIPT OF THIS REQUEST, THE AMERICAN ARBITRATION ASSOCIATION WILL ATTEMPT TO RESOLVE THE DISPUTE. IF THE DISPUTE CANNOT BE RESOLVED, YOUR CASE WILL BE FORWARDED FOR ARBITRATION. IF YOU WISH TO ARBITRATE YOUR CLAIM COMPLETE BOTH SIDES OF THIS FORM TO THE BEST OF YOUR ABILITY. PLEASE PRINT OR TYPE.

APPLICANT FOR BENEFITS			AS ASSIGNEE
LAST NAME	FIRST NAME	ADDRESS	☐ YES ☐ NO
INJURED PERSON			DATE OF ACCIDENT
LAST NAME	FIRST NAME	ADDRESS	
POLICYHOLDER			POLICY NUMBER
LAST NAME	FIRST NAME	ADDRESS	
INSURER OR SELF-INSURER	INSURER'S CLAIMS OFFICE ADDRESS		
INSURER'S REPRESENTATIVE	TELEPHONE NUMBER	CLAIM OR FILE NUMBER	

ACCIDENT LOCATION_____

DESCRIPTION OF ACCIDENT _____

WAS INSURER CONTACTED AFTER CLAIM WAS SUBMITTED?_____

NAME AND TITLE OF PERSON CONTACTED _____

DATE OF LAST CONTACT _____

REASON GIVEN BY INSURER FOR NONPAYMENT OF CLAIM(S) DETAILED ON REVERSE SIDE:_____

_____

_____

REASON YOU BELIEVE THE DENIED OR OVERDUE BENEFITS SHOULD BE PAID_____

_____

SUPPLY DETAILS OF DISPUTE ON REVERSE SIDE

AAA FORM AR

DETAILS OF DISPUTED CLAIM

_____Loss of Earnings: Date claim made:_____   Gross earnings per month:$ _____

Period in dispute: From: _____ To: _____   Amount claimed: $_____

_____Medical (Attach bills in dispute):

DOCTOR, HOSPITAL OR OTHER HEALTH PROVIDER	AMOUNT OF EACH BILL	AMOUNT PAID	UNPAID OR DISPUTED BALANCE	DATES OF SERVICE	DATE BILL MAILED	WAS VERIFICATION REQUESTED		
						NO	YES	DATE SUPPLIED

_____Other Necessary Expense(s) (Attach bills in dispute):

TYPE OF EXPENSE CLAIMED	AMOUNT CLAIMED	DATE INCURRED	DATE MAILED	AMOUNT IN DISPUTE

____DEATH BENEFIT   DATE DEATH CERTIFICATE MAILED TO INSURER:_____

___INTEREST

BENEFIT PAID LATE	AMOUNT OF BILL	DATE MAILED TO INSURER	WAS VERIFICATION REQUESTED?			DATE PAID BY INSURER
			NO	YES	SUPPLIED DATE	

___ATTORNEY'S FEE

ANY PERSON WHO KNOWINGLY AND WITH INTENT TO DEFRAUD ANY INSURANCE COMPANY OR OTHER PERSON FILES AN APPLICATION FOR INSURANCE OR STATEMENT OF CLAIM CONTAINING ANY MATERIALLY FALSE INFORMATION, OR CONCEALS FOR THE PURPOSE OF MISLEADING, INFORMATION CONCERNING ANY FACT MATERIAL THERETO, COMMITS A FRAUDULENT INSURANCE ACT, WHICH IS A CRIME, AND SHALL ALSO BE SUBJECT TO A CIVIL PENALTY NOT TO EXCEED FIVE THOUSAND DOLLARS AND THE STATED VALUE OF THE CLAIM FOR EACH SUCH VIOLATION.

THIS FORM IS SUBSCRIBED AND AFFIRMED
BY THE APPLICANT AS TRUE UNDER THE PENALTY OF PERJURY
THE APPLICANT AFFIRMS THAT A COPY OF THIS COMPLETED FORM HAS BEEN MAILED
TO THE INSURER AGAINST WHOM ARBITRATION IS BEING REQUESTED

ARBITRATION REQUESTED BY:		
LAST NAME FIRST NAME		NAME OF LAW FIRM, IF ANY
TELEPHONE NUMBER		
		ADDRESS
SIGNATURE	ARE YOU AN ATTORNEY? YES NO	DATE

HOW TO FILE

1. MAIL THIS COMPLETED FORM AND ALL REQUESTED ATTACHMENTS IN DUPLICATE TOGETHER WITH A $40.00 FILING FEE PAYABLE TO THE AMERICAN ARBITRATION ASSOCIATION TO:

NEW YORK NO-FAULT CONCILIATION CENTER
AMERICAN ARBITRATION ASSOCIATION
65 BROADWAY
NEW YORK, NEW YORK 10006

2. MAIL A COPY OF THIS FORM TO THE INSURER AGAINST WHOM YOU ARE REQUESTING ARBITRATION AND RETAIN A COPY FOR YOUR RECORDS.

AAA FORM AR (12/99)

APPENDIX 15:
SAMPLE COMPLAINT TO RECOVER NO-FAULT INSURANCE BENEFITS UNDER NEW YORK STATE LAW

[NAME OF COURT]	COMPLAINT
[CAPTION OF CASE]	INDEX NO:

The plaintiff, complaining of the defendant by his attorney, [name of attorney], herein states the following:

1. Upon information and belief, the defendant is a foreign insurance corporation doing business in the State of New York.

2. At all times hereinafter mentioned, the defendant was and still is engaged in the business of insuring automobiles and the drivers thereof against certain hazards, including personal injuries.

3. On [date] the defendant issued and delivered an insurance policy, Policy No.___, to its insured, [name of insured].

4. Said insurance policy contains an agreement to insure the driver of the insured vehicle for "Basic Economic Loss" as described in Insurance Law § 5102(a), up to the limit set forth in the policy.

5. On or about [date of accident], at about [time of accident], and while the policy was in full force and effect, the plaintiff was injured while driving the insured vehicle with the permission of the insured, [name of insured].

6. Solely as a result of the accident and injuries sustained, the plaintiff suffered "Basic Economic Loss", hereinafter referred to as "First Party Benefits".

7. The plaintiff and/or the insured gave notice to the defendant as soon as practicable after the aforementioned accident.

8. On or about [date], some four (#) months after the accident, the defendant sent a letter enclosing a copy of its No-Fault application form to the plaintiff.

9. The plaintiff has completed and properly executed all the forms supplied by the defendant and has submitted the required proof of his claim therewith.

10. Demand has been made of the defendant by the plaintiff for "First Party Benefits" and the defendant has not paid the sum or any part thereof.

11. More than thirty (30) days have elapsed since the accident and since the date of plaintiffs demand. Payments are therefore overdue.

12. That as a result of the above, the plaintiff incurred an uncompensated loss of wages, medical bills, interest, attorneys' fees and was otherwise injured and damaged in the sum of _____ ($_____) Dollars.

WHEREFORE, plaintiff demands judgment against the defendant in the sum of _____ ($_____) Dollars, plus interest, the costs and disbursements of this action, and such other and further relief as the Court deems just and proper.

[Name of Attorney]

Attorney for Plaintiff

[Attorney's Address]

[Attorney's Telephone Number]

Source: McKinney's Selected Consolidated Laws Forms, Volume 26A, West Publishing Company, 1992.

APPENDIX 16:
SAMPLE COMPLAINT FOR PERSONAL INJURY IN AN AUTOMOBILE ACCIDENT UNDER NEW YORK STATE LAW

[NAME OF COURT]   COMPLAINT

[CAPTION OF CASE]   INDEX NO:

The plaintiff, complaining of the defendant by his attorney, [name of attorney], herein states the following:

1. That at all times hereinafter mentioned, the plaintiff was, and still is, a resident of the City of [name], County of [name], New York.

2. That upon information and belief, at all times hereinafter mentioned, and at the time of the commencement of this action, the defendant was, and still is, a resident of the City of [name], County of [name], New York.

3. That upon information and belief, the defendant was, and still is, the owner and operator of [identify defendant's vehicle].

4. That at all times hereinafter mentioned, the plaintiff was lawfully the operator of [identify plaintiff's vehicle].

5. That upon information and belief, at all the times hereinafter mentioned, [identify road upon which accident occurred, e.g. Main Street located at the intersection of Spring Street, in the County of Queens, New York,] was a public highway running in a general north-south direction.

6. That on or about [date and time], plaintiff was lawfully operating his vehicle [describe accident, e.g., which was traveling in a southerly direction along Main Street, when the automobile owned and operated by the defendant, traveling in a northerly direction along Main Street

collided with the plaintiff's vehicle while making a left turn across Main Street at the intersection of Spring Street], causing the injuries to the plaintiff.

7. That the accident and the injuries resulting to the plaintiff were caused solely by reason of the negligence of the defendant.

8. That the defendant was negligent, reckless, and careless at that time and place in that defendant turned left across the road without signalling and without giving any warning of his intention to so turn left across the road; in that the defendant was not paying proper attention to the operation or progress of the vehicle operated by the plaintiff; in that the defendant failed to keep a proper lookout before turning left across the road for danger reasonably to be apprehended and/or to observe and heed road and traffic conditions then and there existing; in that the defendant failed to exercise due and proper care and diligence to avoid the accident; in that defendant was otherwise generally careless and negligent.

9. That as a result of the collision and accident, plaintiff suffered great bodily injuries, and he became sick, sore, lame and disabled and has remained sick, sore, lame and disabled since the accident and has suffered great pain and agony and is informed and believes that he will continue to suffer for a long time to come, and that the injuries are permanent; that the plaintiff has been unable to carry on his duties for some time and believes that in the future he will be unable to, and hindered in, carrying out his duties.

10. That by reason of the foregoing, the plaintiff has been damaged in the sum of [set forth dollar amount of claim].

Plaintiff must set forth the allegations which meet the verbal or economic threshold that take this claim out of nofault using either paragraph 11-A or 11-B, whichever is applicable to the facts:

11-A. That as a result of the foregoing, the plaintiff has sustained a serious injury, as defined in subsection (d) of section 5102 of the Insurance Law of the State of New York.

11-B. That as a result of the foregoing, the plaintiff has sustained economic loss greater than basic economic loss, as defined in subsection (a) of section 5102 of the Insurance Law of the State of New York.

WHEREFORE, plaintiff demands judgment against the defendant in the sum of [set forth dollar amount of claim, plus interest, the costs and disbursements of this action, and such other and further relief as the Court deems just and proper.

[Name of Attorney]

Attorney for Plaintiff

[Attorney's Address]

[Attorney's Telephone Number]

Source: McKinney's Selected Consolidated Laws Forms, Volume 1A, West Publishing Company, 1992.

APPENDIX 17:
SAMPLE APPLICATION FOR NO-FAULT BENEFITS

APPLICANT INFORMATION

1. Name:

2. Address:

3. Home Phone:

4. Business Phone:

5. Date of Birth:

6. Social Security No:

ACCIDENT INFORMATION

1. Date and time of accident:

2. Place of accident:

3. Brief description of accident:

4. Describe injuries:

IDENTIFY VEHICLE YOU OCCUPIED OR OPERATED AT TIME OF ACCIDENT

1. Make/Model/Year of vehicle:

2. Owner of vehicle:

3. Vehicle type (circle one): (a) a bus or school bus; (b) an automobile; (c) a truck; (d) a motorcycle.

4. Applicant's status (circle one): (a) driver; (b) passenger; (c) pedestrian; (d) member of policyholder's household.

5. Does applicant, or a member of applicant's household, own a motor vehicle?

MEDICAL CARE AND EXPENSES

1. Names and addresses of all doctors or other health care providers who rendered care to the applicant:

2(a). Name and address of hospital, if any, where applicant was treated:

2(b). Applicant was an (a) in-patient or (b) out-patient?

2(c). Date of admission:

3. Dollar amount of medical expenses to date:

4. Does applicant expect to undergo further medical care?

LOST EARNINGS

1. Did applicant lose time from work?

2. Date absence from work began:

3. Date applicant returned to work, if applicable:

4. Applicant's average weekly earnings:

5. Number of days in work week:

6. Number of hours per day:

7. Names and addresses of all employers for one-year period prior to accident; occupations; and dates of employment with each employer.

OTHER INFORMATION

1. Detail any other expenses resulting from injury:

2. Is applicant eligible for, or in receipt of, disability benefits?

3. Is applicant eligible for, or in receipt of, worker's compensation benefits?

4. Is applicant eligible for, or in receipt of, medicare benefits?

By signing below, applicant authorizes the insurer to submit any and all of these forms to another party or insurer if necessary to perfect its rights or recovery under the applicable provisions of the no-fault law.

_____

Signature Line and Date

APPENDIX 18:
AUTHORIZATION FOR RELEASE OF MEDICAL RECORDS IN CONNECTION WITH A CLAIM UNDER MOTOR VEHICLE NO-FAULT INSURANCE LAW

This authorization, or a photocopy thereof, will authorize you to furnish all information you may have regarding my condition while under your observation or treatment, including the history obtained, X-ray and physical findings, diagnosis and prognosis. You are authorized to provide this information in accordance with [applicable no-fault law].

Date:_____

Signature Line:_____

Print or type name:

Social Security Number:

APPENDIX 19:
VERIFICATION OF MEDICAL TREATMENT BY ATTENDING PHYSICIAN OR OTHER HEALTH CARE PROVIDER IN CONNECTION WITH A CLAIM UNDER MOTOR VEHICLE NO-FAULT INSURANCE LAW

DATE:

TO: [Name and Address of Health Care Provider]

RE: [Name of Claimant; Name of Policyholder and Policy Number; Date of Accident; Insurance Company File Number]

FROM: [Name of Insurer's Claim Representative; Insurance Company; Address; Phone Number]

Kindly complete and submit this form as soon as possible to facilitate payment of this patient's motor vehicle no-fault benefits.

If you previously submitted an earlier report on this accident, you need only note any changes from the information previously furnished and the additional charges, if any.

PATIENT INFORMATION

1. Name and address:

2. Age:

3. Sex:

4. Occupation:

HEALTH CARE INFORMATION

5. Diagnosis and concurrent conditions:

6. Date symptoms first appeared:

7. Date of patient's first consultation for condition:

8. Has patient ever had same or similar condition? If so, give date and details:

9. Is patient's condition solely a result of the above-referenced automobile accident? If no, explain.

10. Is patient's condition due to injury arising out of patient's employment?

11(a) Will patient's injury result in significant disfigurement or permanent disability? (Circle one)

   (i) Yes

   (ii) No

   (iii) Not determinable at this time.

11(b) If your answer was yes, give details.

12. Dates patient was disabled and unable to work:

13. If patient is still disabled, give date by which patient should be able to return to work:

14. Will the patient require rehabilitation and/or occupational therapy as a result of the injuries sustained in this accident? If yes, describe the recommended treatment.

15. Provide details of services rendered to date, including (a) date of service; (b) address where service was rendered; (c) description of service rendered; (d) fee schedule/treatment code;(e) charges for each service rendered; and total charges to date.

16. Has the patient received, or is the patient entitled to Medicare benefits for the above-described treatment?

17. Is the patient still under your care for the same condition?

18. Will health services likely be required for more than one year from the date of the accident?

19. Estimated duration of future treatment:

Date:___

[Health Care Provider's Signature]

Taxpayer Identification Number:

APPENDIX 20:
VERIFICATION OF HOSPITAL TREATMENT IN CONNECTION WITH A CLAIM UNDER MOTOR VEHICLE NO-FAULT INSURANCE LAW

DATE:

TO: [Name and Address of Hospital]

RE: [Name of Policyholder; Policy Number; Date of Accident; Insurance Company File Number]

FROM: [Name of Insurer's Claim Representative; Insurance Company; Address; Phone Number]

Kindly complete and submit this form as soon as possible to facilitate payment of this patient's motor vehicle no-fault benefits.

PATIENT INFORMATION

1. Patient Name:

2. Patient Address:

3. Date of Birth

ADMISSION AND TREATMENT INFORMATION

4. Date of Admission:

5. Time of Admission:

6. Date of Discharge:

7. Time of Discharge:

8(a) Admission Diagnosis:

8(b) Discharge Diagnosis:

9. Is patient's condition due to injury arising out of patient's employment?

10. Describe operations and/or procedures performed:

11. Was treatment rendered solely as a result of the above-referenced accident? If no, explain.

12. Is the patient still under your care for the same condition?

13. Services Rendered:

NOTE: HOSPITAL CHARGES MUST BE COMPUTED IN ACCORDANCE WITH RATES PERMITTED BY [APPLICABLE STATUTE]:

In-Patient Care:

Ward: [#] days [$] rate per day = $

Semi-Private: [#] days [$] rate per day = $

Private: [#] days [$] rate per day = $

Intensive Care Unit: [#] days [$] rate per day = $

Extended Care Facility: [#] days [$] rate per day = $

Other In-Patient Care (describe and itemize): $

    TOTAL IN-PATIENT CHARGES = $

Out-Patient Care (describe and itemize):

    TOTAL OUT-PATIENT CHARGES = $

      GRAND TOTAL: $

      LESS MEDICARE PAYMENTS: $

      BALANCE: $

Date:

By:_____

Print or type name signed above

Title:

Telephone Number:

APPENDIX 21:
AUTHORIZATION FOR RELEASE OF EMPLOYMENT INFORMATION IN CONNECTION WITH A CLAIM UNDER MOTOR VEHICLE NO-FAULT INSURANCE LAW

This authorization, or a photocopy thereof, will authorize you to furnish all information you may have regarding my wages, salary or other losses while employed by you. You are authorized to provide this information in accordance with [applicable no-fault law].

Date:_____

Signature Line:_____

Print or type name:

Social Security Number:

APPENDIX 22:
EMPLOYER WAGE VERIFICATION REPORT IN CONNECTION WITH A CLAIM UNDER MOTOR VEHICLE NO-FAULT INSURANCE LAW

DATE:

TO: [Name and Address of Employer]

RE: [Name of Employee; Social Security Number of Employee; Name of Policyholder and Policy Number; Date of Accident; Insurance Company File Number]

FROM: [Name of Insurer's Claim Representative; Insurance Company; Address; Phone Number]

Dear Employer:

The above-named person has applied for benefits under [applicable no-fault law] as a result of injuries sustained in a motor vehicle accident on the date indicated. We understand this person is your employee or former employee. To assist us in determining benefits that may be due the applicant, please provide us with the answer to the questions listed below.

Please complete and submit this form to my attention as soon as possible to facilitate payment of lost earnings.

Thank you for your cooperation.

By:_____

[Claims Representative]

1. Employee's Occupation:

2. Dates of Employment:

3. Gross earnings during 52 week period prior to accident: $

4. Wage or salary on date of accident (check one):

    (a) Hourly—$

    (b) Weekly—$

    (c) Monthly—$

5. Number of hours worked per day:

6. Number of days worked per week:

7. Dates absent from work following accident:

8(a) Has employee received, or is employee entitled to receive, benefits under any workers compensation law as a result of this accident? (check one)

    (i) Yes

    (ii) No

    (iii) Undetermined

8(b) Address and policy number of workers compensation insurer:

9(a) Has employee received, or is employee entitled to receive, disability benefits as a result of this accident? (check one)

    (i) Yes

    (ii) No

    (iii) Undetermined

9(b) Address and policy number of disability insurer:

10(a) Was or will employee be paid by employer for this absence from work? (check one)

    (i) Yes

    (ii) No

10(b) How much was or will employee be paid?

10(c) Will the employee lose accumulated leave time as a result of this payment?

Date:

By:_____

Print or type name signed above

Title:

Telephone Number:

Employer Federal Identification Number:

APPENDIX 23:
VERIFICATION OF SELF-EMPLOYMENT INCOME IN CONNECTION WITH A CLAIM UNDER MOTOR VEHICLE NO-FAULT INSURANCE LAW

DATE:

TO: [Name and Address of Applicant]

RE: [Name of Policyholder and Policy Number; Date of Accident; Insurance Company File Number]

FROM: [Name of Insurer's Claim Representative; Insurance Company; Address; Phone Number]

Dear Applicant:

The information requested below will be used by the above insurer to determine the amount of loss of earnings from work, if any, to which you may be entitled as a result of this accident. Therefore, it would be in your best interests to complete the form and submit all documents requested to the best of your ability.

1. Your Occupation:

2. Business Address:

3. Business Telephone:

4. Nature of Business or Profession:

5. Dates you were unable to attend to your business or profession due to this accident:

6(a) Did you hire anyone to substitute for you while you were absent due to your injuries? (check one)

    (i) Yes

(ii) No

6(b) If yes, please complete the following:

(i) Name, address and telephone number of substitute:

(ii) Period for which substitute employed:

(iii) Wage or salary paid and state whether paid daily, weekly or monthly: $_____ per _____ .

(iv) Gross amount paid to substitute: $_____

7(a) If answer to question #6(a) was Yes, did you suffer a net loss of earnings from work in addition to the cost of substitute service? (check one)

(i) Yes

(ii) No

7(b) If yes, state the amount of net loss claimed for the period described in question #5: $_____

8(a) If your answer to question #6(a) was No, did you suffer a net loss of earnings from work during your claimed disability? (check one)

(i) Yes

(ii) No

8(b) If yes, state the amount of net loss claimed for the period described in question #5: $_____

9. In order for us to properly evaluate your claim, it is essential that you submit copies of your Federal Income Tax returns for the last two years. In addition, submit whatever documents are available to prove your income for the current year. If you have not filed either of the tax returns, submit whatever proof of earnings you have for those years which you feel will assist us in evaluating your claim. If we are unable to verify your loss of earnings from the documents submitted, additional documentation will be required.

THIS FORM IS SUBSCRIBED AND AFFIRMED BY THE APPLICANT AS TRUE UNDER THE PENALTIES OF PERJURY.

Date:_____

BY: [Signature of Applicant]

APPENDIX 24:
AGREEMENT TO PURSUE SOCIAL SECURITY DISABILITY BENEFITS IN CONNECTION WITH A CLAIM UNDER MOTOR VEHICLE NO-FAULT INSURANCE LAW

DATE:

TO: [Name and Address of Applicant]

RE: [Name of Policyholder and Policy Number; Date of Accident; Insurance Company File Number]

FROM: [Name of Insurer's Claim Representative; Insurance Company; Address; Phone Number]

Dear Applicant:

This form must be completed by you and your district Social Security office in order for your no-fault loss of earnings benefits to continue without interruption.

I, [name of applicant], agree to apply for and diligently pursue, within [#] days from the date of this letter, Social Security Disability benefits that may be recoverable on account of injuries caused by the above-referenced accident.

I further agree to reimburse the Insurer for any amounts that may have been or may be advanced by the Insurer pursuant to this agreement, pending receipt of Social Security Disability benefits. I may deduct from the reimbursement any attorney fees which I have paid in order to obtain social Security benefits.

The Insurer, [name of insurer], upon receipt of this agreement and the below authorization for release of information by the Social Security Administration, both duly signed by the applicant, or the applicant's legal guardian, agrees to continue the payment of no-fault benefits as permitted by [applicable no-fault insurance law] until such Social Security Disability benefits are received.

In the event that the applicant fails to sign and return this agreement and authorization, or to apply for social Security Disability benefits in accordance with the agreement within the aforesaid time period, the insurer shall estimate the amount of monthly Social Security Disability benefits which it believes the applicant would be entitled to receive and, beginning on [date], the Insurer shall deduct the estimated Social Security Disability benefits from loss of earnings benefits due on account of injuries caused by this accident to the applicant.

Date:_____

_____

BY: [Signature of Applicant]

Date:_____

_____

BY: [Signature of Insurer's Representative]

_____

AUTHORIZATION FOR RELEASE OF INFORMATION BY THE SOCIAL SECURITY ADMINISTRATION

Name of Claimant:

Social Security Claim Number:

Date:

I hereby authorize the Social Security Administration to disclose the necessary information, such as my name, account number, disability benefit rate and date of entitled to benefits to the person or agency listed below:

Disclose information to: [Name and address of Insurer]

This authorization is effective for only as long as is needed to determine my eligibility to benefits and my rate of benefit payment.

Date:_____

_____

BY: [Signature of Claimant]

APPENDIX 25:
AUTO CHOICE REFORM ACT OF 2001
(H.R.1704)

SECTION 1. SHORT TITLE AND TABLE OF CONTENTS.

(a) SHORT TITLE—This Act may be cited as the 'Auto Choice Reform Act of 2001'.

(b) TABLE OF CONTENTS—The table of contents for this Act is as follows:

Sec. 1. Short title and table of contents.

Sec. 2. Findings and purposes.

Sec. 3. Definitions.

Sec. 4. Auto choice insurance system.

Sec. 5. Personal injury protection system.

Sec. 6. Tort maintenance system.

Sec. 7. Protection against insurance fraud.

Sec. 8. Source of compensation in cases of accidental injury.

Sec. 9. Preservation of State and private rights.

Sec. 10. Applicability to States.

SECTION 2. FINDINGS AND PURPOSES

(a) FINDINGS—The Congress finds the following:

(1) Auto insurance premiums are too high, largely because the current auto liability insurance system (referred to in this subsection as the 'present system')—(A) encourages costly fraudulent claims and unnecessarily contentious behavior by both claimants and defendants; and (B) often requires expensive lawyers on both sides of a dispute to settle claims.

(2) The adversarial tort system that is in effect in 35 States poorly compensates the most needy individuals, in that the system—(A) pays no liability benefits to more than 30 percent of all accident victims; (B) takes too long to pay victims when it does pay them; (C)(i) pays victims with minor injuries an average of two to three times the cost of their medical bills and lost wages; but (ii) pays victims with serious injuries an average of less than 50 percent of those bills and lost wages; and (D) pays twice as much for plaintiff and defense lawyers combined as it pays for victims' medical bills and lost wages.

(3) The chance of winning the lawsuit lottery in the present system—(A) results in the filing of billions of dollars of fraudulent or otherwise unnecessary auto insurance claims annually; (B) generates billions of dollars in unnecessary health care costs for private, Federal, and State health care programs; (C) raises auto insurance premiums for all drivers, including drivers operating business vehicles; and (D) makes auto insurance premiums unaffordable for many low—income individuals.

(4) The present system harms cities by—(A) encouraging the filing of frivolous and inflated claims that cities pay at the expense of all taxpayers; and (B) contributing to the abandonment of cities by taxpayers who can achieve substantial reductions in their auto insurance premiums by moving to the suburbs.

(5) The present system provides individuals little incentive to purchase safer automobiles.

(6) All of the no—fault insurance reform laws that exist in 13 States provide more timely and equitable compensation for medical bills and lost wages to more accident victims.

(7) Some of those no—fault insurance reform laws, however, have not been successful in controlling insurance premiums, in large part because opponents of such reform have weakened the laws by creating loopholes for unnecessary and costly lawsuits.

(8) The alternative form of insurance, personal injury protection, that may be offered to drivers by reason of this Act, gives drivers the ability to—(A)(i) insure themselves in all accidents for their own medical bills and lost wages; and (ii) sue other drivers on the basis of fault for any economic losses that are not covered by their insurance; and (B) forgo lawsuits against other drivers for noneconomic damages on the basis of fault in return for being free from suit for noneconomic damages by other drivers.

(9) Personal injury protection, by reducing the need for auto liability lawsuits and the incentives for fraudulent and otherwise questionable

claims, could—(A) save drivers billions of dollars annually; and (B) enable them to receive more adequate and timely compensation when they are seriously injured.

(10) Personal injury protection would benefit society by—(A) increasing respect for the law by eliminating the incentives of the adversarial present system for fraudulent claims and unnecessarily contentious behavior by both claimants and defendants; (B) saving precious health care resources; (C) making it more affordable for low—income individuals to operate an automobile to get to better paying jobs; (D) reducing the incentives for individuals to abandon cities, by providing greater savings for drivers who reside in cities; (E) freeing city taxpayers' dollars for reductions in taxes or expanded city programs by reducing the amount of frivolous and unnecessary lawsuits against cities; (F) encouraging drivers to own safer automobiles by giving insurers the opportunity to reduce premiums for the owners of safe automobiles; and (G) helping to free up court dockets that are currently overburdened with personal injury lawsuits fueled by the incentives for lawsuits under the present system.

(11) A new auto insurance system that allows drivers to select the form of auto insurance that best meets their needs, by choosing between—(A) a modified version of the present system, or (B) the personal injury protection system described in paragraph (9),would enable drivers to reduce the cost of auto insurance, increase the amount of average compensation in the event of a serious accident, and enhance individual freedom.

(12) The Federal Government should encourage consumer choice, but not exercise regulatory authority over the business of auto insurance, including rates and insurer solvency, as that authority is appropriately exercised by the States.

(13) During the period beginning January 1, 1957, and ending December 31, 1996—(A) the Federal Government spent more than $400 billion to facilitate highway construction in the United States; and (B) hundreds of thousands of individuals have been killed in motor vehicle accidents on highways constructed with those funds.

(14) The auto insurers who operate in interstate commerce pay greater than 70 percent of the compensation paid to accident victims.

(15) Through programs such as medicare, medicaid, and social security, the Federal Government pays a significant amount of the costs for compensating motor vehicle accident victims.

(16) It is necessary and proper for the Congress, in the exercise of its authority to establish post roads and regulate commerce under section

8 of article I of the Constitution, to provide drivers throughout the United States with an alternative to address the problems of the adversarial present system and the inadequate no—fault insurance reforms.

(b) PURPOSES— The purposes of this Act are as follows:

(1) To enable consumers of auto insurance to choose between two insurance systems, which are—(A) a tort maintenance system based on applicable State law that provides for substantially similar insurance premiums and compensation for injuries as compared to the auto insurance system in existence in that State on the date of enactment of this Act; and (B) a personal injury protection system that compensates accident victims directly for their medical bills and lost wages with substantially less need to pursue lawsuits and provides the opportunity for—

(i) substantial reductions in auto insurance premiums;

(ii) more comprehensive recovery of medical bills and lost wages in a shorter period of time; and

(iii) the right to sue negligent drivers for any uncompensated medical bills or lost wages.

(2) To preserve the rights of States to regulate the business of auto insurance.

SECTION 3. DEFINITIONS.

In this Act:

(1) ACCIDENT—The term 'accident' means an unforeseen or unplanned event that—(A) causes injury; and (B) arises from the operation, maintenance, or use of a motor vehicle.

(2) ADD—ON LAW—The term 'add—on law' means a State law that provides that persons injured in motor vehicle accidents—(A) are compensated without regard to fault for economic loss; and (B) have the right to claim without any limitation for noneconomic loss based on fault.

(3) COLLATERAL SOURCE—The term 'collateral source' means a person, other than a tortfeasor or a motor vehicle insurer, that has a legal obligation to pay compensation for economic loss to a person who is injured in an accident.

(4) COMMON CARRIER—The term 'common carrier' means a motorized vehicle of any kind, licensed for highway use, that is—(A) required

to be registered under the provisions of applicable State law relating to motor vehicles; and (B) used in the business of transporting persons.

(5) ECONOMIC LOSS—The term 'economic loss' means objectively verifiable pecuniary loss caused by an accident for—(A) reasonable and necessary medical and rehabilitation expenses; (B) loss of earnings; (C) funeral costs; and (D) replacement services loss.

(6) ELECTRONIC SIGNATURE—The term 'electronic signature' means any letters, characters, or symbols executed or adopted by a party with an intent to authenticate a writing that are—(A) manifested by—

(i) electronic means; or

(ii) any other similar means; and (B) logically associated with that writing.

(7) FINANCIAL RESPONSIBILITY LAW—The term 'financial responsibility law' means a law (including a law requiring compulsory coverage) penalizing motorists for failing to carry defined limits of tort liability insurance covering motor vehicle accidents.

(8) FIRST PARTY BENEFITS—The term 'first party benefits' means benefits paid or payable by an insurer to an insured of that insurer under a personal injury protection policy or a tort maintenance coverage policy applicable to that insured.

(9) INJURY—The term 'injury' means bodily injury, sickness, disease, or death.

(10) INSURER—The term 'insurer' means any person who is engaged in the business of issuing or delivering motor vehicle insurance policies (including an insurance agent, if appropriate) under applicable State law.

(11) MOTOR CARRIER—The term 'motor carrier' means—

(A) a person who—

(i) transports by motor vehicle goods for another person or entity for compensation; and

(ii) is liable for the operation of the vehicle under part 387 of title 49, Code of Federal Regulations; or

(B) a person who transports such person's goods by a motor vehicle that such person owns or leases.

(12) MOTOR VEHICLE—The term 'motor vehicle' means a vehicle with 4 or more wheels licensed for highway use that is required to be regis-

tered under the provisions of the applicable State financial responsibility law relating to motor vehicles.

(13) NAMED INSURED—The term 'named insured' means a person designated by name in a personal injury protection policy or tort maintenance coverage policy as the insured.

(14) NO—FAULT MOTOR VEHICLE LAW—The term 'no—fault motor vehicle law' means a State law that provides that—(A) persons injured in motor vehicle accidents are paid compensation without regard to fault for their economic loss that results from injury; and (B) in return for the payment referred to in subparagraph (A), claims based on fault, including claims for noneconomic loss, are limited to a defined extent.

(15) NONECONOMIC LOSS—The term 'noneconomic loss' means subjective, nonmonetary losses recognized under applicable State tort law.

(16) OCCUPY—The term 'occupy' means, with respect to the operation, maintenance, or use of a motor vehicle, to be in or on a motor vehicle or to be engaged in the immediate act of entering into or alighting from a motor vehicle.

(17) OPERATION, MAINTENANCE, OR USE OF A MOTOR VEHICLE—

(A) The term 'operation, maintenance, or use of a motor vehicle' means any activity involving or related to the transportation by a motor vehicle.

(B) Such term includes occupying or being engaged in the immediate act of entering into or alighting from a motor vehicle before or after its use for transportation.

(C) Such term does not include—(i) conduct within the course of a business of manufacturing, sale, repairing, servicing, or otherwise maintaining motor vehicles, unless the conduct occurs outside the scope of the business activity; or (ii) conduct within the course of loading or unloading a motor vehicle, unless the conduct occurs while occupying or being engaged in the immediate act of entering into or alighting from a motor vehicle before or after its use for transportation.

(18) PERSON—The term 'person' means any individual, corporation, company, association, firm, partnership, society, joint stock company, or any other entity, including any governmental entity.

(19) PERSONAL INJURY PROTECTION—The term 'personal injury protection' means insurance that provides for—(A) benefits to a personal injury protection insured for economic loss without regard to fault for

injury resulting from a motor vehicle accident in accordance with this Act; (B) a waiver of tort claims against other drivers, other than—

(i) claims for uncompensated economic loss based on fault; and

(ii) other tort claims exempted from such a waiver under this Act; (C) coverage against claims for uncompensated economic losses based on fault by another party that is entitled to recover those losses under this Act; and (D) coverage against claims for economic or noneconomic losses of a third party with respect to which the recovery of those losses is not covered under this Act.

(20) PERSONAL INJURY PROTECTION INSURED—The term 'personal injury protection insured' means a person covered by the form of insurance described in section 5.

(21) PERSONAL INJURY PROTECTION INSURER—The term 'personal injury protection insurer' means an insurer who is engaged in the business of providing personal injury protection.

(22) PERSONAL INJURY PROTECTION SYSTEM—The term 'personal injury protection system' means the insurance system described in section 5.

(23) REPLACEMENT SERVICES LOSS—The term 'replacement services loss' means expenses reasonably incurred in obtaining ordinary and necessary services from other persons who are not members of the injured person's household, in lieu of the services the injured person would have performed for the benefit of the household.

(24) RESIDENT RELATIVE OR DEPENDENT—

(A) The term 'resident relative or dependent' means a person—(i) who is related to the named insured by blood, marriage, adoption, or otherwise (including a dependent receiving financial services or support from such insured); and (ii) who—

(I) resides in the same household as the named insured at the time of the accident; or

(II) usually makes a home in the same family unit as the named insured, even though that person may temporarily live elsewhere.

(B) Such term does not include any person who maintains or is required to maintain insurance for a motor vehicle that such person owns.

(25) STATE—The term 'State' includes the District of Columbia, the Commonwealth of Puerto Rico, Guam, the United States Virgin Islands,

American Samoa, the Commonwealth of the Northern Mariana Islands, the Trust Territories of the Pacific Islands, and any other territory or possession of the United States.

(26) TORT LIABILITY—The term 'tort liability' means the legal obligation to pay damages for an injury in an accident adjudged to have been caused by a tortfeasor, under applicable State law.

(27) TORT LIABILITY INSURANCE—The term 'tort liability insurance' means a contract of insurance under which an insurer agrees to pay, on behalf of an insured, damages that the insured is obligated to pay to a third person because of the liability of the insured to that person.

(28) TORT MAINTENANCE COVERAGE—The term 'tort maintenance coverage' means insurance coverage under which a tort maintenance insured, if involved in an accident with a personal injury protection insured, may recover first party benefits for economic and noneconomic losses from the insurer of that insured, based on fault under applicable State law.

(29) TORT MAINTENANCE INSURED—The term 'tort maintenance insured' means a person covered by the form of insurance described in section 6.

(30) TORT MAINTENANCE SYSTEM—The term 'tort maintenance system' means an insurance system described in section 6.

(31) UNCOMPENSATED ECONOMIC LOSS—

(A) The term 'uncompensated economic loss' means any objectively verifiable pecuniary loss payable based on fault under applicable State tort law, except for any such loss that is determined by a court of competent jurisdiction to be, in whole or in part, a product of fraudulent activity by the person making the claim.

(B) Such term includes a reasonable attorney's fee calculated on the basis of the time actually expended and the value of the attorney's efforts as reflected in payment to the attorney's client, other than any attorney's fees when the uncompensated economic loss is attributable only to a deductible for coverage specified in subparagraph (C)(i).

(C) Subject to section 8(j)(2), such term does not include amounts paid or payable under—(i) personal injury protection; (ii) tort maintenance coverage; (iii) no—fault or add—on motor vehicle insurance; (iv) Federal, State, or private disability or sickness programs; (v) Federal, State, or private health insurance programs; (vi) employer wage continuation programs; or (vii) workers' compensation or similar occupational compensation laws.

(32) UNINSURED MOTORIST—The term 'uninsured motorist' means the owner of a motor vehicle, including the resident relatives or dependents of the owner, who is uninsured under either the personal injury protection system described in section 5 or the tort maintenance system described in section 6—(A) at the limits prescribed by the applicable State financial responsibility law; or (B) an amount prescribed under section 5(a)(1).

SECTION 4. AUTO CHOICE INSURANCE SYSTEM.

(a) OPERATION OF THE RIGHT TO CHOOSE—

(1) IN GENERAL—Under this Act, an insurer may offer a choice between—(A) the personal injury protection system described in section 5; and (B) the tort maintenance system described in section 6.

(2) ELECTION BY SELF—INSURED PERSONS—A self—insured person, as determined under an applicable State law, may elect coverage under paragraph (1) by filing a notice with the appropriate State or Federal agency.

(3) EFFECT OF ELECTION BY ELECTRONIC MEANS—For purposes of making an election of an insurance system under this subsection, unless prohibited by applicable State law, an electronic signature shall have the same force and effect as a handwritten signature.

(b) EFFECT OF CHOICE ON RESIDENT RELATIVES OR DEPENDENTS—

(1) IN GENERAL—Except as provided in paragraph (2), a person who chooses either the personal injury protection system or the tort maintenance system also binds the resident relatives or dependents of that person.

(2) EXCEPTION—An adult resident relative or dependent of a person described in paragraph (1) may select the form of insurance that such person does not select if the adult resident relative or dependent makes that selection expressly in writing to the insurer.

(3) TERMS AND CONDITIONS—Insurers may specify reasonable terms and conditions governing the commencement, duration, and application of thechosen coverage, depending on the number of motor vehicles and owners of such vehicles in a household.

(c) UNIFORMITY RULES—

(1) IN GENERAL—Notwithstanding subsection (b)(2) and in order to minimize conflict between the insurance options, an insurer may maintain and apply underwriting rules that encourage uniformity in the provision of insurance benefits within a household.

(2) UNIFORMITY IN INSURANCE IN EMPLOYMENT—Except as provided in paragraph (6), an employer that elects an insurance option described in subparagraph (A) or (B) of subsection (a)(1) binds the employees of that employer for purposes of coverage of that employee in the course of employment by that employer.

(3) UNIFORMITY IN INSURANCE FOR MOTOR CARRIERS—Except as provided in paragraph (6), a motor carrier that elects an insurance option described in subparagraph (A) or (B) of subsection (a)(1) binds any owner, operator, or occupant of a motor vehicle operated by that motor carrier.

(4) UNIFORMITY IN INSURANCE FOR COMMON CARRIERS—Except as provided in paragraph (6), an owner of a common carrier that elects an insurance option described in subparagraph (A) or (B) of subsection (a)(1) binds the owner and any operator or occupant of that common carrier.

(5) UNIFORMITY IN INSURANCE FOR MOTOR VEHICLE RENTALS—

(A) IN GENERAL—Except as provided in subparagraph (B), a person who is engaged in the business of renting motor vehicles and who elects an insurance option described in subparagraph (A) or (B) of subsection (a)(1) binds any operator or occupant of the rented motor vehicle with respect to the operation of that vehicle.

(B) EXCEPTION—Subparagraph (A) shall not apply if a customer who rents a motor vehicle—

(i) specifically elects to obtain coverage within the rental agreement other than the coverage elected by the person engaged in the business of renting the motor vehicle; and

(ii) pays a separate charge for that optional coverage.

(6) RIGHT OF EMPLOYEES, OPERATORS, AND CERTAIN OCCUPANTS TO PURCHASE ADDITIONAL COVERAGE—

(A) EMPLOYEES—An employee under paragraph (2) may elect to purchase separate personal injury protection or tort maintenance coverage in excess of the insurance provided by the employer in the scope of the employment of that employee.

(B) OPERATORS AND OCCUPANTS OF MOTOR CARRIERS—An operator or occupant of a motor carrier under paragraph (3) may elect to purchase separate personal injury protection or tort maintenance coverage in excess of the insurance provided to that operator or occupant by the motor carrier as an operator or occupant of that motor carrier.

(C) OPERATORS AND OCCUPANTS OF COMMON CARRIERS—An operator or occupant of a common carrier under paragraph (4) may elect to purchase separate personal injury protection or tort maintenance coverage in excess of the insurance provided to that operator or occupant by the owner of the common carrier as an operator or occupant of the common carrier.

(D) EFFECT OF ELECTION—The election by an employee, operator, or occupant to purchase insurance coverage under this paragraph shall not affect the liability of an employer, motor carrier, or common carrier.

(d) FAILURE TO ELECT TYPE OF INSURANCE—

(1) IN GENERAL—Except as provided in subsection (b)(1), any person who fails to elect a type of insurance under subsection (a)(1) shall be deemed to have elected insurance under the tort maintenance system in effect in the State of that person's residence.

(2) RULE OF CONSTRUCTION—This subsection shall not be construed to prevent a State from enacting a law that deems a person who fails to elect a type of insurance under this section to have elected insurance under the personal injury protection system.

(e) CONSUMER INFORMATION PROGRAM—

(1) STATE PROGRAM—The State official charged with jurisdiction over insurance rates for motor vehicles may establish and maintain a program designed to ensure that consumers are adequately informed concerning—

(A) the comparative cost of insurance under the personal injury protection system and the tort maintenance system; and

(B) the benefits, rights, and obligations of insurers and insureds under each such system.

(2) INSURER PROGRAM—An insurer that offers a choice of insurance systems under subsection (a)(1) shall provide to each consumer, before that consumer chooses motor vehicle insurance, written consumer information to ensure that consumers are adequately informed about—(A) the comparative cost of insurance under the personal injury protection system and the tort maintenance system; and (B) the benefits, rights, and obligations of insurers and insureds under each system.

(3) ADEQUATE NOTICE—If an insurer files consumer information forms under paragraph (2) with the State official charged with jurisdiction over insurance rates for motor vehicles and such forms are not dis-

approved within a reasonable period of time after that filing, such filing and use of the information in accordance with paragraph (2) shall be presumed to be adequate notice.

(f) SUPERSEDING PROVISION—Subject to section 10, this Act supersedes a State law to the extent that the State law is otherwise inconsistent with the requirements of this Act.

SECTION 5. PERSONAL INJURY PROTECTION SYSTEM.

(a) MINIMUM POLICY REQUIREMENTS—In order to constitute a personal injury protection policy covered by this Act, a motor vehicle insurance policy issued by an insurer shall, at a minimum—

(1) for each accident, provide personal injury protection benefits to each personal injury protection insured in amounts equal to—(A) the minimum per—person limits of liability insurance for personal injury under the relevant State financial responsibility law applicable to private passenger vehicles; or (B) in a State covered by a no—fault motor vehicle law, the minimum level of insurance required for no—fault benefits;

(2) contain provisions for a waiver of tort claims against drivers other than the insured, except—(A) claims for uncompensated economic loss based on fault; or (B) other tort claims exempted from such a waiver under this Act;

(3) contain provisions for third party liability coverage in amounts equal to the minimum limits required under applicable Federal or State financial responsibility law for—(A) property damage; and (B) bodily injury to cover—

(i) uncompensated economic losses for parties who are entitled to recover such losses under this Act; and

(ii) economic and noneconomic losses of third parties whose recovery is not affected by this Act.

(b) PRIMACY OF PAYMENT—

(1) IN GENERAL—

(A) PERSONAL INJURY PROTECTION BENEFITS—

(i) IN GENERAL—Except as provided in subparagraph (B), in any case in which a personal injury protection insurer and a collateral source are obligated to pay benefits for the same economic loss under this Act, the personal injury protection insurer shall be liable for the primary payment of benefits to cover that economic loss.

(ii) LIABILITY OF COLLATERAL SOURCES—A collateral source shall be liable for economic loss only to the extent that the loss exceeds benefits paid or payable by an insurer under an applicable personal injury protection insurance policy.

(B) EXCEPTION—Personal injury protection benefits shall be reduced by an amount equal to any benefits provided or required to be provided under—

(i) an applicable Federal or State law for workers' compensation;

(ii) any State—required nonoccupational disability insurance; or

(iii) any occupational disability insurance covering professional drivers of motor vehicles who are independent contractors.

(2) REIMBURSEMENT OF PAYORS—

(A) IN GENERAL—A personal injury protection insurer may take appropriate measures to ensure that any person otherwise eligible for personal injury protection benefits who has been paid or is being paid for losses payable by personal injury protection from a source other than the applicable personal injury protection insurer shall not receive multiple payment for those losses.

(B) ACCRUAL OF RIGHTS—Any right to payment for losses referred to in subparagraph (A) from a personal injury protection insurer accrues only to that payor. Payments by a payor referred to in subparagraph (A) shall not be counted against personal injury limits for personal injury protection until such time as the payor is reimbursed under this subparagraph.

(3) PROTECTION AGAINST DUPLICATION—Upon receipt of reasonable notice, a personal injury protection insurer shall reimburse a collateral source for payments made by that collateral source for economic loss for injury resulting from a motor vehicle accident, to the extent that the personal injury protection insurer is obligated to pay for that economic loss.

(c) PROMPT AND PERIODIC PAYMENT—

(1) IN GENERAL—A personal injury protection insurer may pay personal injury protection benefits periodically as losses accrue.

(2) LATE PAYMENT—Except as provided in section 7, a personal injury protection insurer that does not pay a claim for personal injury protection benefits during the 30—day period beginning on the date on

which that insurer receives a submission of reasonable proof of the loss for which those benefits are payable, shall pay—(A) the loss compounded at a rate of 24 percent per annum as liquidated damages; and (B) a reasonable attorney's fee calculated on the basis of the time actually expended or the value of the attorney's efforts as reflected in payment to the attorney's client.

(3) ADMINISTRATION OF PERSONAL INJURY PROTECTION BENEFITS—To the extent consistent with this Act, any applicable provision of a State nofault motor vehicle law or add—on law governing the administration of payment of benefits without reference to fault shall apply to the payment of benefits under personal injury protection under this subsection.

(d) AUTHORIZATIONS FOR DEDUCTIONS AND EXCLUSIONS—

(1) IN GENERAL—A personal injury protection insurer may write personal injury protection—(A)(i) without any deductible; or (ii) subject to a reasonable deductible; and (B) with an exclusion of coverage for first party benefits to cover the losses of the personal injury protection insured caused by that insured's—

   (i) driving under the influence of alcohol or illegal drugs; or

   (ii) driving while seeking to intentionally injure another person.

(2) APPLICABILITY OF DEDUCTIBLES—The deductibles and exclusions described in paragraph (1) shall apply only to—(A) the person named in the applicable insurance policy; and (B) the resident relatives or dependents of the person described in subparagraph (A).

SECTION 6. TORT MAINTENANCE SYSTEM.

(a) MINIMUM POLICY REQUIREMENTS—

(1) IN GENERAL—The coverage for a person who chooses insurance under section 4(a)(1)(B) shall include—(A) the type of motor vehicle insurance that is otherwise required under applicable State law; and (B) tort maintenance coverage at a level that is at least equivalent to the level of insurance required under the applicable State financial responsibility law for bodily injury liability.

(2) RESPONSIBILITY FOR PAYMENT UNDER TORT MAINTENANCE COVERAGE—The responsibility for payment for any claim under tort maintenance coverage is assumed by the insurer of the tort maintenance insured to the extent of such coverage.

(b) ADDITIONAL PAYMENTS FROM UNINSURED MOTORIST COVERAGE AND UNDERINSURED MOTORIST COVERAGE—A tort maintenance insured who also purchases an insurance policy that provides uninsured motorist coverage or underinsured motorist coverage may recover under the terms of that policy for any economic or noneconomic loss arising from an accident involving a personal injury protection insured, in any case in which the amount of those economic or noneconomic losses exceed the aggregate amount recovered or recoverable from the—

(1) tort maintenance coverage of the tort maintenance insured; and

(2) personal injury protection insured.

SECTION 7. PROTECTION AGAINST INSURANCE FRAUD.

(a) TIMELY SUBMISSION OF CLAIMS FOR FIRST PARTY BENEFITS—

(1) No insurer shall be obligated to pay first party benefits to a personal injury protection insured for any economic loss that occurred more than 60 days prior to the submission of a claim for such loss.

(2) The time for submission of a claim shall be tolled during any period during which the insured can show that—

(A) the insured was physically unable—(i) to submit proof of the claim; or (ii) to supply the identity of the insurer to the provider of services; or

(B) the insured was unable to identify the insurer despite good faith efforts to do so.

(b) LOSS OF FIRST PARTY BENEFITS—No insurer shall be obligated to pay any first party benefits to a personal injury protection insured for any economic loss that a court of competent jurisdiction determines is, in whole or in part, the product of fraudulent activity by the insured with respect to an accident.

(c) LOSS OF ENTITLEMENT TO PURCHASE INSURANCE—An insurer may cancel, decline to renew, or refuse to issue a personal injury protection policy to any person who a court of competent jurisdiction has determined has engaged in fraudulent activity with respect to an accident during the previous three years.

SECTION 8. SOURCE OF COMPENSATION IN CASES OF ACCIDENTAL INJURY.

(a) ACCIDENTS INVOLVING PERSONS CHOOSING THE TORT MAINTENANCE SYSTEM—

(1) IN GENERAL—A tort maintenance insured who is involved in an accident with another person shall be subject to applicable State law

for injury, except that, based on fault, that person may, upon submission of proof of insurance—(A) recover from any personal injury protection insured for uncompensated economic loss (and not for noneconomic loss); and (B) be liable to a personal injury protection insured for uncompensated economic loss (and not for noneconomic loss).

(2) ALLOCATION OF TORT MAINTENANCE PAYMENTS—In determining the extent of recovery of a tort maintenance insured from a personal injury protection insured under subsection (b), the payments made to the tort maintenance insured from tort maintenance coverage shall first be allocable to economic loss, and any remainder may be allocable to noneconomic loss.

(b) ACCIDENTS INVOLVING PERSONS CHOOSING THE PERSONAL INJURY PROTECTION SYSTEM—

(1) RIGHT TO RECOVER ECONOMIC LOSS—A personal injury protection insured who is injured in an accident may recover under the policy of that insured only for economic loss, without regard to fault.

(2) RIGHT TO SUE FOR UNCOMPENSATED ECONOMIC LOSS BASED ON FAULT—A personal injury protection insured who is involved in an accident with a tort maintenance insured, or another personal injury protection insured, may recover based on fault from that other insured for uncompensated economic loss (and not for noneconomic loss).

(c) ALLOCATION OF COMPARATIVE FAULT—In any case in which a claim is made under this Act for uncompensated economic loss on the basis of comparative fault under applicable State law, the recovery of damages shall be based on the percentage of fault with respect to the amount of uncompensated economic loss.

(d) ACCIDENTS INVOLVING PERSONS CHOOSING THE PERSONAL INJURY PROTECTION SYSTEM AND PERSONS WHO ARE UNLAWFULLY UNINSURED—

(1) RIGHTS OF PERSONAL INJURY PROTECTION INSUREDS—A personal injury protection insured who is involved in an accident with an uninsured motorist—(A) shall be compensated under the insured person's policy for economic loss without regard to fault; and (B) may recover from the uninsured motorist (other than under uninsured or underinsured motorist coverage) for economic loss and for noneconomic loss based on fault.

(2) LIMITATIONS ON LAWSUITS BY UNINSURED MOTORISTS—An uninsured motorist may not recover from a personal injury protection insured for noneconomic loss.

(e) ACCIDENTS INVOLVING MOTORISTS UNDER THE INFLUENCE OF ALCOHOL OR ILLEGAL DRUGS OR INFLICTING INTENTIONAL INJURY—Notwithstanding any other provision of this Act, a personal injury protection insured who is in an accident may—

(1) recover all damages based on fault under applicable State law from a person who—(A) at the time of the accident, was driving under the influence of alcohol or illegal drugs (as those terms are defined under applicable State law); or (B) caused an injury while seeking to intentionally injure another person; and

(2) be liable for all damages based on fault under applicable State law, if such insured—(A) at the time of the accident, was driving under the influence of alcohol or illegal drugs (as those terms are defined under applicable State law); or (B) caused an injury while seeking to intentionally injure another person.

(f) RIGHTS OF LAWFULLY UNINSURED PERSONS—Nothing in this Act shall be construed to affect the tort rights or obligations of any person lawfully uninsured under the terms of an applicable State law for insurance under either the personal injury protection system or tort maintenance system under section 4(a)(1).

(g) RIGHTS OF PERSONS OCCUPYING MOTOR VEHICLES WITH FEWER THAN FOUR LOAD—BEARING WHEELS—Nothing in this Act shall be construed to affect the tort rights or obligations of a person who occupies a motor vehicle with fewer than 4 load—bearing wheels or an attachment thereto, unless an applicable contract for personal injury protection under which that person is insured specifies otherwise. The preceding sentence applies without regard to whether the person is otherwise legally insured for personal injury protection or tort maintenance coverage.

(h) FORFEITURE OF FRAUDULENT CLAIMS—An owner, operator, or occupant of a motor vehicle involved in an accident forfeits the right to make a claim against an insured motorist for economic or noneconomic loss resulting from injury incurred by that owner, operator, or occupant if that owner, operator, or occupant knowingly participated in a scheme to obtain insurance payments for any accident that was staged with the intent to commit insurance fraud.

(i) PRIORITY OF BENEFITS—

(1) IN GENERAL—Except as provided in paragraph (2), a personal injury protection insured or a tort maintenance insured may recover first party benefits only under the coverage of that insured in effect at the time of the accident.

(2) EXCEPTIONS—

(A) IN GENERAL—Except as provided in subparagraph (B), with respect to an accident that occurred while an injured individual was occupying a motor vehicle—

(i) furnished by an employer, the primary coverage shall be the coverage applicable to the motor vehicle; or

(ii) that was being used in the business of transporting individuals or property, the primary coverage shall be the coverage applicable to that motor vehicle.

(B) CERTAIN CLAIMANTS—A claimant may claim first party benefits in an amount greater than the amounts determined under the limits under the primary insurance coverage described in clause (i) or (ii) of subparagraph (A), if that claimant would otherwise be able to receive those increased benefits by reason of insurance coverage of that claimant that would otherwise apply, but for the operation of subparagraph (A).

(j) REIMBURSEMENT RIGHTS OF PERSONAL INJURY PROTECTION INSURERS AND COLLATERAL SOURCES—

(1) REIMBURSEMENT RIGHTS OF PERSONAL INJURY PROTECTION INSURERS—

(A) IN GENERAL—A personal injury protection insurer may seek reimbursement under subparagraph (B), from—

(i) an uninsured motorist who is liable for damages caused by the accident;

(ii) a motorist who was under the influence of alcohol or illegal drugs at the time of the accident and whose conduct was the proximate cause of the accident;

(iii) a person who caused an injury while seeking to intentionally injure another person; or

(iv) any other person who is not affected by the limitations on tort rights and liabilities under this Act and whose conduct was the proximate cause of the accident.

(B) REIMBURSEMENT—A personal injury protection insurer may seek reimbursement under this subparagraph to the extent of the obligations of that insurer, with respect to payments for a personal injury protection insured of that insurer with respect to an accident caused in whole or in part, as determined in accordance with applicable State law, from a person referred to in subparagraph (A), for the losses that insurer—

(i) has paid or reimbursed; or

(ii) under applicable law, is obligated to pay.

(2) REIMBURSEMENT RIGHTS OF COLLATERAL SOURCES—With respect to an accident, a collateral source may seek reimbursement from an insurer in a civil action based on fault.

(3) PROHIBITION ON MULTIPLE RECOVERY—In any action to recover losses arising out of an accident, a person may not recover or introduce into evidence in a civil action against another person any amount of a loss that a collateral source or personal injury protection insurer—(A) has paid or reimbursed; or (B) is obligated to pay.

(k) CHOICE OF LAW—

(1) APPLICABLE LAW—With respect to a claim relating to a motor vehicle accident involving persons from different States, the choice—of—law principles applicable under the law of the State of competent jurisdiction shall apply.

(2) APPLICABLE COVERAGE IN AN AUTO CHOICE STATE—With respect to an accident that involves a person from a State in which this Act does not apply and a person from a State in which this Act applies, in any case in which the accident occurs in a State in which this Act applies, the coverage of the person from the State in which this Act does not apply shall be deemed to be the form of insurance (whether personal injury protection or tort maintenance coverage) that most closely reflects the form of insurance that the person maintains in the State of residence of the person.

(l) JURISDICTION—This Act shall not confer jurisdiction on the district courts of the United States under section 1331 or 1337 of title 28, United States Code.

(m) STATUTES OF LIMITATIONS—

(1) IN GENERAL—Subject to paragraph (2), nothing in this Act shall supersede an applicable State law that imposes a statute of limitations for claims related to an injury caused by an accident, except that such statute shall be tolled during the period during which any personal injury protection or tort maintenance coverage benefits are paid.

(2) CLAIMS—Unless otherwise provided by State law, a claim for personal injury protection benefits under this Act shall be filed not later than two years after the economic loss that is the subject of the claim is incurred.

(n) LIMITATIONS ON NONRENEWAL, CANCELLATION, AND PREMIUM INCREASES—An insurer shall not cancel, decline to renew, or increase the premium of a person insured by the insurer solely because that insured person or any other injured person made a claim for—

(1) personal injury protection benefits; or

(2) tort maintenance coverage benefits in any case in which there is no basis for ascribing fault to the insured or one for whom the insured is vicariously liable.

(o) NEGLIGENT DRIVER RATINGS—Nothing in this Act shall be construed to limit insurers from canceling, failing to renew, or increasing premiums for an insured person if there is a basis for ascribing moving traffic violations or fault for an accident caused by that insured or any resident relative or dependent, or employee of that insured.

(p) IMMUNITY—

(1) IN GENERAL—Except as provided in paragraph (2), no insurer, insurance agent or broker, insurance producer representing a motor vehicle insurer, automobile residual market plan, or attorney licensed to practice law within a State, or any employee of any such person or entity, shall be liable in an action for damages on account of—(A) an election of—

(i) the tort maintenance system under section 4(a)(1)(B); or

(ii) the personal injury protection system under section 4(a)(1)(A); or (B) a failure to make a required election.

(2) EXCEPTION—Paragraph (1) shall not apply in any case in which—

(A) a person described in that paragraph—

(i) willfully and intentionally misrepresents the insurance choices available to a customer or client of that person; or

(ii) willfully and with the intent to defraud, induces the election of one motor vehicle insurance system described in paragraph (1)(A) over the other motor vehicle insurance system described in that paragraph; and

(B) the misrepresentation or inducement under subparagraph (A) was the proximate cause of that customer or client's electing or failing to make an election of an insurance system under subparagraph (A) or (B) of section 4(a)(1).

SECTION 9. PRESERVATION OF STATE AND PRIVATE RIGHTS.

(a) RIGHTS OF STATES—Nothing in this Act shall be construed—

(1) to waive or affect any defense of sovereign immunity asserted by any State under any law or by the United States;

(2) to preempt State choice—of—law rules with respect to claims brought by a foreign nation or a citizen of a foreign nation;

(3) to affect the right of any court to transfer venue, to apply the law of a foreign nation, or to dismiss a claim of a foreign nation or of a citizen of a foreign nation on the ground of inconvenient forum;

(4) to preclude a State from establishing a schedule of payments for medical protocols for treatment of an injury that arises from an accident;

(5) to preclude a State from requiring personal injury protection insurers to offer first party insurance that establishes a dollar value for noneconomic loss in objectively verifiable defined classes of cases involving death or serious and permanent bodily injury;

(6) to preclude a State from enacting a law applicable to all motor vehicle accident cases, including cases covered by this Act, to establish a minimum dollar value for economic losses for defined classes of cases involving death or serious bodily injury;

(7) to preclude a State from providing that forms of insurance other than those listed in section 5(b) shall be subtracted from personal injury protection insurance benefits otherwise payable for injury; or

(8) to preclude a State from enacting a law that—(A) allows litigation by tort maintenance insureds against personal injury protection insureds for economic and noneconomic loss; and (B) assures through a reallocation device that the advantage of tort claim waivers by personal injury protection insureds against tort maintenance insureds is reflected in the premiums of personal injury protection insureds.

(b) PRESERVATION OF STATE REGULATORY AUTHORITY—Nothing in this Act may be construed—

(1) to preclude a State or State official charged with regulatory authority over the business of insurance from fully exercising that regulatory authority, including adopting regulations and procedures regarding—(A) rates; (B) policy forms; (C) company solvency; (D) consumer protection; (E) underwriting and marketing practices; and (F) carrying out the requirements of this Act; or

(2) to allow or provide for Federal regulation of motor vehicle insurance.

(c) RIGHTS OF PRIVATE PARTIES—Nothing in this Act may be construed—

(1) to require a personal injury protection insurer to offer, or a personal injury protection insured to purchase, any coverage for bodily injury in addition to the coverage required under this Act, including uninsured motorist coverage, underinsured motorist coverage, or coverage for medical payments;

(2) to prevent insurers and insureds from contracting to limit recovery for the loss of earnings under personal injury protection by—(A) limiting such recovery to only 60 percent or more of lost wages or income; (B) limiting the amount of such recovery payable per week; or (C) limiting the period of time after an accident during which the benefits referred to in this paragraph are payable to a period of not less than one year;

(3) to prevent insurers and insureds from contracting—(A) to limit recovery for economic loss for medical and rehabilitation expenses to the average amount actually paid for a particular course of treatment; or (B) to provide medical or rehabilitation services through designated health care providers;

(4) to prevent an insurer from contracting with insureds, as permitted by applicable State law, to have submitted to arbitration any dispute with respect to payment of personal injury protection or tort maintenance coverage;

(5) to affect the worker classification of a person, either as an employee or an independent contractor, on the basis of the election of an employer or motor carrier of an insurance system under section 4(a); or

(6) to affect the awarding of punitive damages, or damages for bad faith refusal to pay a claim, under any applicable State law.

SECTION 10. APPLICABILITY TO STATES.

(a) ELECTION OF NONAPPLICABILITY BY STATES—Subject to subsections (c) through (e), this Act shall apply with respect to a State, unless—

(1) by not later than the earlier of the date that is one year after the date of enactment of this Act or the expiration of the first regular legislative session of the State beginning after the date of enactment of this Act, the State enacts a statute that—(A) cites the authority of this subsec-

tion; (B) declares the election of that State that this Act shall not apply with respect to that State; and (C) contains no other provision; or

(2)(A) the State official charged with jurisdiction over insurance rates for motor vehicles makes a finding that this Act does not apply by reasons of the applicability of the conditions described in subsection (b)(1)(A); and

(B) that finding is made and any review described in subsection (b)(1)(B) is completed not later than the date specified in subsection (b)(1)(C).

(b) NONAPPLICABILITY BASED ON STATE FINDING—

(1) IN GENERAL—This Act shall not apply with respect to a State, if—

(A) the State official charged with jurisdiction over insurance rates for motor vehicles makes a finding that the statewide average motor vehicle premiums for bodily injury insurance in effect immediately before the date of enactment of this Act will not be reduced by an average of at least 30 percent for persons choosing the personal injury protection system, in the amounts required under section 5 (without including in the calculation for personal injury protection insureds any costs for uninsured, underinsured, or medical payments coverages);

(B) the finding described under subparagraph (A) is supported by evidence adduced in a public hearing and reviewable under the applicable State administrative procedure law; and

(C) the finding described under subparagraph (A) is made, and any review of such finding under subparagraph (B) is completed, not later than 120 days after the date of enactment of this Act.

(2) COMPARISON OF BODILY INJURY PREMIUMS—For purposes of making a comparison under paragraph (1)(A) of premiums for personal injury protection with preexisting premiums for bodily injury insurance (in effect immediately before the date of enactment of this Act), the preexisting bodily injury insurance premiums shall include premiums for—

(A) bodily injury liability, uninsured and underinsured motorists' liability, and medical payments coverage; and

(B) if applicable, no-fault benefits under a no-fault motor vehicle law or add-on law.

(c) IMPLEMENTATION PERIOD—Except as provided in subsection (d), if a State fails to enact a law by the applicable date specified in paragraph (1) of subsection (a) or if a finding described in paragraph (2) of that subsection is not made and reviewed by the date specified in subsection (b)(1)(C), this Act shall apply to that State beginning on the date that is 270 days after the later of those dates.

(d) ACCELERATED APPLICABILITY—

(1) IN GENERAL—Subject to paragraph (2), a State may enact a law that provides for the implementation of the provisions of this Act in that State before an otherwise applicable date determined under subsection (a).

(2) APPLICABILITY—If a State makes an election under paragraph (1), this Act shall apply to that State beginning on the date that is 270 days after the date of such election.

(e) ELECTION OF NONAPPLICABILITY BY A STATE AFTER THIS ACT BECOMES APPLICABLE WITH RESPECT TO THE STATE—After this Act becomes applicable with respect to a State under subsection (c) or (d), this Act shall cease to apply with respect to that State if the State enacts a statute that meets the requirements of subparagraphs (A) through (C) of subsection (a)(1).

GLOSSARY

Abolish—To repeal or revoke, such as a law or custom.

Accident—An unforeseen event, occurring without intent or design on the part of the person whose act caused it.

Action—A judicial proceeding whereby one party prosecutes another for a wrong done, for protection of a right, or prevention of a wrong.

Actionable—Giving rise to a cause of action.

Actionable Negligence—The breach or nonperformance of a legal duty through neglect or carelessness, resulting in damage or injury to another.

Actual Damages—Actual damages are those damages directly referable to the breach or tortious act, and which can be readily proven to have been sustained, and for which the injured party should be compensated as a matter of right.

Affirmative Defense—In a pleading, a matter constituting a defense.

Aggrieved Party—One who has been injured, suffered a loss, or whose legal rights have been invaded by the act of another.

Allegation—Statement of the issue that the contributing party is prepared to prove.

Answer—In a civil proceeding, the principal pleading on the part of the defendant in response to the plaintiff's complaint.

Assumption of Risk—The legal doctrine that a plaintiff may not recover for an injury to which he assents.

Automobile Liability Insurance—Refers to protection in case others hold you legally responsible for bodily injury and/or damage to property losses incurred as the result of a motor vehicle accident.

Bodily Injury Liability Insurance (BI)—Bodily Injury Liability Insurance refers to insurance coverage for injuries to other people when the insured vehicle's driver is legally at fault.

Burden of Proof—The duty of a party to substantiate an allegation or issue to convince the trier of fact as to the truth of their claim.

Cause of Action—The factual basis for bringing a lawsuit.

Civil Action—An action maintained to protect a private, civil right as opposed to a criminal action.

Civil Court—The court designed to resolve disputes arising under the common law and civil statutes.

Collision Coverage—Collision coverage refers to insurance coverage when the insured's car is damaged as a result of colliding with another object—a brick wall, for example, or a rollover. This insurance applies only to the car and is usually optional unless the car is leased or financed in which case the lender would require collision coverage to protect itself from losses.

Compensatory Damages—Compensatory damages are those damages directly referable to a breach or tortious act, and which can be readily proven to have been sustained, and for which the injured party should be compensated as a matter of right.

Complaint—In a civil proceeding, the first pleading of the plaintiff setting out the facts on which the claim for relief is based.

Comprehensive Coverage—Comprehensive coverage refers to insurance coverage when the insured's car is stolen or damaged in ways that don't involve a collision — e.g., fire, theft, vandalism, etc. This coverage is usually optional unless the car is leased or financed in which case the lender would require collision coverage to protect itself from losses.

Conflict of Law—The body of law by which the court in which the action is pending chooses which law to apply in a controversy, where there exists diversity between the applicable law of two jurisdictions, both of which have an interest.

Contributory Negligence—The act or omission amounting to want of ordinary care on the part of the complaining party which, concurring with the defendant's negligence, is the proximate cause of his or her injury.

Court—The branch of government responsible for the resolution of disputes arising under the laws of the government.

Culpable—Referring to conduct, it is that which is deserving of moral blame.

Damages—In general, damages refers to monetary compensation which the law awards to one who has been injured by the actions of another, such as in the case of tortious conduct or breach of contractual obligations.

Declarations Page—The Declarations page is the first page of the insurance policy that generally includes the insured's name, address, the insured property, its location and description, the policy period, the amount of insurance coverage, the premiums and additional specific information provided by the insured.

Deductible—The deductible is the insured's out-of-pocket expense that the insured agrees to pay for losses under a certain dollar amount. For example, if the policy deductible is $500 and the damage is $750, the insured must pay $500 and the insurance carrier will pay the balance of $250.

Defendant—In a civil proceeding, the party responding to the complaint.

Defense—Opposition to the truth or validity of the plaintiff's claims.

Duty—The obligation, to which the law will give recognition and effect, to conform to a particular standard of conduct toward another.

Economic Benefits—Economic benefits are tangible, out-of-pocket expenses, such as medical expenses, rehabilitation expenses, lost wages and essential services.

Fact Finder—In a judicial or administrative proceeding, the person, or group of persons, that has the responsibility of determining the acts relevant to decide a controversy.

Fact Finding—A process by which parties present their evidence and make their arguments to a neutral person, who issues a nonbinding report based on the findings, which usually contains a recommendation for settlement.

Family Purpose Doctrine—The doctrine which holds the owner of a family car liable in tort when it is operated negligently by another member of the family.

Financial Responsibility Law—A financial responsibility law is a law that requires motorists to have automobile insurance.

Foreseeability—A concept used to limit the liability of a party for the consequences of his or her acts, to consequences that are within the scope of a foreseeable risk.

Injury—Any damage done to another's person, rights, reputation or property.

Insurance—A contingency agreement, supported by consideration, whereby the insured receives a benefit, e.g. money, in the event the contingency occurs.

Intentional Tort—A tort or wrong perpetrated by one who intends to do that which the law has declared wrong, as contrasted with negligence in which the tortfeasor fails to exercise that degree of care in doing what is otherwise permissible.

Joint and Several—The rights and liabilities shared among a group of people individually and collectively.

Judge—The individual who presides over a court, and whose function it is to determine controversies.

Judgment—A judgment is a final determination by a court of law concerning the rights of the parties to a lawsuit.

Judgment Proof—Refers to the status of an individual who does not have the financial resources or assets necessary to satisfy a judgment.

Jurisdiction—The power to hear and determine a case.

Jury—A group of individuals summoned to decide the facts in issue in a lawsuit.

Jury Trial—A trial during which the evidence is presented to a jury so that they can determine the issues of fact, and render a verdict based upon the law as it applies to their findings of fact.

Lex Loci Contractus—Law of the place where the contract was made.

Lex Loci Delecti—Law of the place where the alleged injury occurred.

Liability—Liability refers to one's obligation to do or refrain from doing something, such as the payment of a debt.

McCarran-Ferguson Act—This law was enacted by Congress in 1945, to grant authority to the states to tax and regulate the business of insurance.

Medical Payments Coverage (MP or MedPay)—Medical payments coverage refers to insurance coverage for doctor bills, hospital bills, and funeral expenses for injuries to the insured and to members of the insured's family who live with the insured, regardless of who caused the accident.

Monetary Threshold—In some "no-fault" states, the monetary or economic threshold refers to a dollar amount for medical and rehabilitation expenses that must be reached in order to file a lawsuit for damages for non-economic damages (i.e. pain and suffering) against the driver who caused the accident. For example, New York's economic threshold is $50,000.

Negligence—The failure to exercise the degree of care which a reasonable person would exercise given the same circumstances.

Negligence Per Se—Conduct, whether of action or omission, which may be declared and treated as negligence without any argument or proof as to the particular surrounding circumstances, because it is contrary to the law.

No-Fault Laws—The insurance laws which provide compensation to any person injured as a result of an automobile accident, regardless of fault.

Non-Economic Benefits—Non-economic benefits refers to intangible benefits, such as pain and suffering, inconvenience, emotional stress, impairment of quality of life, and loss of consortium.

Personal Injury Protection (PIP)—Personal injury protection refers to a package of medical benefits that provides broad protection for medical costs, lost wages, loss of essential services normally provided by the injured person, and funeral costs.

Plaintiff—In a civil proceeding, the one who initially brings the lawsuit.

Pleadings—Refers to plaintiff's complaint which sets forth the facts of the cause of action, and defendant's answer which sets forth the responses and defenses to the allegations contained in the complaint.

Preferred Provider Organization (PPO)—This is an option available in some jurisdictions whereby an insured can agree to use a specific PPO for medical treatment for injuries sustained in an automobile accident in return for lower premiums.

Prima Facie Case—A case which is sufficient on its face, being supported by at least the requisite minimum of evidence, and being free from palpable defects.

Property Damage Liability (PD)—Property damage liability refers to insurance coverage available if the insured damages another's property—e.g., car, fence, building, etc.

Regulation—The insurance industry is state-regulated. State insurance laws are administered by insurance departments whose job includes approval of rates and policy forms, investigation of company practices, review of annual financial statements, periodic examination of books and liquidation of insolvent insurers.

Release—A document signed by one party, releasing claims he or she may have against another party, usually as part of a settlement agreement.

Service of Process—The delivery of legal court documents, such as a complaint, to the defendant.

Settlement—An agreement by the parties to a dispute on a resolution of the claims, usually requiring some mutual action, such as payment of money in consideration of a release of claims.

Statute of Limitations—Any law which fixes the time within which parties must take judicial action to enforce rights or thereafter be barred from enforcing them.

Survival Statute—A statute that preserves for a decedent's estate a cause of action for infliction of pain and suffering and related damages suffered up to the moment of death.

Third party—In an insurance contract, a third party is anyone other than the policyholder and the family members covered under the insurance policy, who are referred to as the first party. The insurance company is the second party in the contract. Anyone else is a third party.

Threshold—The threshold is the set limit which, if met, allows the injured person to file a lawsuit to attempt to be paid for damages for bodily injury, such as "pain and suffering," from the driver who caused the accident.

Tort—A private or civil wrong or injury, other than breach of contract, for which the court will provide a remedy in the form of an action for damages.

Tortfeasor—A wrongdoer.

Tortious Conduct—Wrongful conduct, whether of act or omission, of such a character as to subject the actor to liability under the law of torts.

Trial—The judicial procedure whereby disputes are determined based on the presentation of issues of law and fact. Issues of fact are decided by the trier of fact, either the judge or jury, and issues of law are decided by the judge.

Trial Court—The court of original jurisdiction over a particular matter.

Underinsured Motorist Coverage (UM)—Underinsured motorist coverage compensates the insured person and other passengers in the vehicle when they're injured as the result of an accident where the at-fault driver is uninsured, underinsured or a hit-and-run.

Verbal Threshold—The verbal threshold is a description of the type of serious injury a person must sustain before being able to file a lawsuit for damages for bodily injury against the driver who caused the accident.

Verdict—The definitive answer given by the jury to the court concerning the matters of fact committed to the jury for their deliberation and determination.

Wrongful Death Statute—A statute that creates a cause of action for any wrongful act, neglect, or default that causes death.

BIBLIOGRAPHY AND ADDITIONAL RESOURCES

Black's Law Dictionary, Fifth Edition. St. Paul, MN: West Publishing Company, 1979.

Gifis, Steven H. *Barron's Law Dictionary, Second Ed.*. Woodbury, NY: Barron's Educational Series, Inc., 1984.

Insurance Institute for Highway Safety. (Date Visited: January 2002) <http://www.hwysafety.org/>.

Insurance News Network (Date Visited: January 2002) <http://www.insure.com/>.

Joost, Robert H. *Automobile Insurance and No-Fault Law 2d*. New York, NY: Clark Boardman Callaghan, 1992 & Supplement 1995.

King, Josephine Y. *No-Fault Automobile Accident Law*. New York, NY: John Wiley & Sons, Inc., 1987.

Summary of Selected State Laws and Regulations Relating to Automobile Insurance. New York, NY: American Insurance Association, Inc., 1986.

Woodruff, M. G., Fonseca, John R., Squillante, Alphonse M. *Automobile Insurance & No-Fault Law*. Rochester, NY: The Lawyers Cooperative Publishing Co., 1974 & Supplement 1991.

United States Bureau of Transportation Statistics. (Date Visited: January 2002) <http://www.bts.gov/>.

United States Department of Transportation. (Date Visited: January 2002) <http://www.dot.gov/>.